Nestlé Toll House best-ever cookies

your history

with Nestlé probably dates to when you were a kid snitching chocolate morsels while your mom baked cookies. Now, *Nestlé Best-Ever Cookies* gives you the simple pleasure of sharing warm, freshly baked treats with your own family.

Like the famous no-fail Nestlé® Toll House® Cookies, these recipes, developed and tested in the Nestlé Culinary Center, guarantee batch after batch of sweet goodness year-round: drop cookies, bars, brownies, slice-and-bake cookies, pies, tarts, cakes and more. Best of all, you probably have the necessary ingredients stocked in your pantry.

Like you, generations of cooks have clipped the Nestlé® Toll House® Cookie recipe from its signature Nestlé packaging. This special book is filled with new and classic recipes that you can use for years to come. And look the other way when your children or grandchildren "steal" a few morsels. That's a tradition, too.

Left: Pumpkin Spiced and Iced Cookies
(see recipe, page 111)
Right: Chunky Chocolate Chip Peanut Butter Cookies
(see recipe, page 35)

contents

Your search is over for fabulous delights ideal for parties or desserts.

Pull off a show-stopping finale at your next party.

Celebrate the comforts of fresh-from-the-oven breads, rolls, muffins and more.

The Nestlé Culinary Center shares its secrets.

Pictured on Cover: Original Nestlé® Toll House® Chocolate Chip Cookies, Double Chocolate Dream Cookies, Macadamia Nut White Chip Pumpkin Cookies, Choc-Oat-Chip Cookies, White Chip Orange Cookies and Oatmeal Scotchies™ (See index for page numbers.)

Copyright© 1998 Nestlé USA, Inc. All rights reserved.
Produced by Meredith® Books, 1716 Locust St., Des Moines, Iowa 50309-3023.
Library of Congress Catalog Card Number: 98-66559
ISBN: 0-696-20904-7 Printed in the United States of America.

the legendary Nestlé®
Toll House® cookie

The Nestlé® Toll House® Cookie got its name from a lovely old tollhouse located between Boston and New Bedford, Massachusetts. Built in 1709, the house had long been a haven for weary travelers in search of food, drink and a change of horses.

In 1930, Mr. and Mrs. Wakefield purchased the historic old house and turned it into the now-famous Toll House Inn. In keeping with tradition, Mrs. Wakefield baked for her guests, perfecting and improving upon many old recipes. Soon, her tasty desserts attracted people from all over New England.

One day, while stirring together a batch of Butter Drop Do cookies, a favorite Colonial recipe, Mrs. Wakefield cut a bar of Nestlé® Semi-Sweet Chocolate into bits and added them to her cookie dough, expecting them to melt. Instead, the chocolate held its shape, softening to a creamy texture. This delicious discovery was dubbed the Nestlé® Toll House® Cookie, which became a widespread favorite. With Mrs. Wakefield's permission, Nestlé put the recipe on the wrapper of the Nestlé® Semi-Sweet Chocolate Bar.

As the popularity of the Nestlé® Toll House® Cookie increased, the company looked for ways to make this cookie easier to bake. First, Nestlé produced a special, scored chocolate bar that could be divided into small sections. Then the company began offering tiny pieces of chocolate in convenient packages—and that's how the first Real Nestlé® Toll House® Semi-Sweet Chocolate Morsels were introduced.

Since they were first created for the Nestlé® Toll House® Cookie, Nestlé® Semi-Sweet Chocolate Morsels have satisfied the chocolate cravings of millions. Today, they're used to make hundreds of delectable chocolate goodies all across America.

Original Nestlé® Toll House® Chocolate Chip Cookies (see recipe, page 8)

original Nestlé® Toll House® chocolate chip cookies

2¼ cups all-purpose flour
1 teaspoon baking soda
1 teaspoon salt
1 cup butter or margarine, softened
¾ cup granulated sugar
¾ cup packed brown sugar
1 teaspoon vanilla extract
2 eggs
2 cups (12-ounce package) NESTLÉ® TOLL HOUSE® Semi-Sweet Chocolate Morsels
1 cup chopped walnuts

COMBINE flour, baking soda and salt in small bowl. Beat butter, granulated sugar, brown sugar and vanilla extract in large mixer bowl until creamy. Add eggs one at a time, beating well after each addition. Gradually beat in flour mixture. Stir in morsels and walnuts. Drop by rounded tablespoon onto ungreased baking sheets.

BAKE in preheated 375°F. oven for 9 to 11 minutes or until golden brown. Let stand for 2 minutes; remove to wire racks to cool completely. Makes about 5 dozen cookies.

Pictured on the cover and on pages 7 and 116.

cookie variations

Although the Original Nestlé® Toll House® Cookie traditionally is a drop cookie, you can enjoy the same delicious flavor in bars and in slice-and-bake cookies with these two easy variations.

Bar Cookie Variation:

PREPARE dough as *on opposite page*. Spread into greased 15 x 10-inch jelly-roll pan. Bake in preheated 375°F. oven for 20 to 25 minutes or until golden brown. Cool completely in pan on wire rack. Cut into bars. Makes 4 dozen.

Pictured on pages 36 and 37.

Slice-and-Bake Cookie Variation:

PREPARE dough as *on opposite page*. Divide in half; wrap each half in waxed paper. Chill for 1 hour or until firm. Shape each half into 15-inch log; wrap in waxed paper. Chill for 30 minutes.* Cut into ½-inch-thick slices; place on ungreased baking sheets. Bake in preheated 375°F. oven for 8 to 10 minutes or until golden brown. Let stand for 2 minutes; remove to wire racks to cool completely. Makes about 5 dozen cookies.

*Note: Logs may be stored in refrigerator for up to 1 week or in freezer for up to 8 weeks.

cookie jar traditions

many a cherished

memory is captured in that cookie jar on

the counter, where little hands reached in

again and again for just one more

irresistible treat. Inspiring delighted smiles

and childhood memories of sweet aromas

drifting from the oven, the traditional

recipes in this chapter are some of Nestlé's

most requested and enjoyed.

Milk Chocolate Oatmeal Cookies (see recipe, page 12),
Frosted Maple Pecan White Chip Cookies (see recipe,
page 13) and Chocolate Peanut Cookies
(see recipe, page 16)

milk chocolate oatmeal cookies

1 1/4 cups all-purpose flour
1/2 teaspoon baking powder
1/2 teaspoon baking soda
1/2 teaspoon ground cinnamon
1/4 teaspoon salt
3/4 cup (1 1/2 sticks) butter or margarine, softened
3/4 cup packed brown sugar
1/3 cup granulated sugar
1 1/2 teaspoons vanilla extract
1 egg
2 tablespoons milk
2 cups (11 1/2-ounce package) NESTLÉ® TOLL HOUSE® Milk Chocolate Morsels
1 cup quick or old-fashioned oats
1/2 cup raisins (optional)

COMBINE flour, baking powder, baking soda, cinnamon and salt in small bowl. Beat butter, brown sugar, granulated sugar and vanilla extract in large mixer bowl until creamy. Beat in egg. Gradually beat in flour mixture and milk. Stir in morsels, oats and raisins. Drop by rounded tablespoon onto ungreased baking sheets.

BAKE in preheated 375°F. oven for 10 to 14 minutes or until edges are crisp but centers are still soft. Let stand for 2 minutes; remove to wire racks to cool completely. Makes about 3 dozen.

Pictured on pages 10 and 11.

frosted maple pecan white chip cookies

3 cups all-purpose flour
2 teaspoons baking soda
2 cups packed brown sugar
1 cup shortening
½ cup (1 stick) butter or margarine, softened
2 eggs
1 teaspoon maple flavoring
1 teaspoon vanilla extract
2 cups (12-ounce package) NESTLÉ® TOLL HOUSE® Premier White Morsels
½ cup chopped pecans
Maple Frosting (recipe follows)
About 60 pecan halves (3½ to 4 ounces)

COMBINE flour and baking soda in medium bowl. Beat brown sugar, shortening, butter, eggs, maple flavoring and vanilla extract in large mixer bowl until creamy. Gradually beat in flour mixture. Stir in morsels and chopped pecans. Drop by rounded tablespoon onto ungreased baking sheets.

BAKE in preheated 350°F. oven for 9 to 12 minutes or until light golden brown. Let stand for 2 minutes; remove to wire racks to cool completely. Spread with Maple Frosting; top each cookie with pecan half. Makes about 5 dozen cookies.

For Maple Frosting:
COMBINE 4 cups powdered sugar, 4 to 6 tablespoons milk, ¼ cup softened butter and 1 teaspoon maple flavoring in medium bowl; stir until smooth.

Pictured on pages 10 and 11.

macadamia nut
white chip pumpkin cookies

  2   cups all-purpose flour
  2   teaspoons ground cinnamon
  1   teaspoon ground cardamom
  1   teaspoon baking soda
  1   cup (2 sticks) butter or margarine, softened
  ½   cup granulated sugar
  ½   cup packed brown sugar
  1   cup LIBBY'S® Solid Pack Pumpkin
  1   egg
  2   teaspoons vanilla extract
  2   cups (12-ounce package) NESTLÉ® TOLL HOUSE® Premier
      White Morsels
  ⅔   cup coarsely chopped macadamia nuts or walnuts, toasted

COMBINE flour, cinnamon, cardamom and baking soda in small bowl. Beat butter, granulated sugar and brown sugar in large mixer bowl until creamy. Beat in pumpkin, egg and vanilla extract until well mixed. Gradually beat in flour mixture. Stir in morsels and macadamia nuts. Drop by rounded tablespoon onto greased baking sheets; flatten slightly with back of spoon or greased bottom of glass dipped into granulated sugar.

BAKE in preheated 350°F. oven for 11 to 14 minutes or until centers are set. Cool for 2 minutes; remove to wire racks to cool completely. Makes about 4 dozen cookies.

Also pictured on the cover and page 19.

Chocolate Mint Brownie Cookies (see recipe, page 17) and
Macadamia Nut White Chip Pumpkin Cookies (see recipe above)

chocolate peanut cookies

2 bars (2 ounces *each*) NESTLÉ® TOLL HOUSE® Semi-Sweet Baking Chocolate Bars, broken into pieces
1¼ cups all-purpose flour
¾ teaspoon baking soda
½ teaspoon salt
½ cup (1 stick) butter or margarine, softened
½ cup packed brown sugar
¼ cup granulated sugar
2 teaspoons vanilla extract
1 egg
1½ cups coarsely chopped honey-roasted peanuts

MICROWAVE baking bars in small, microwave-safe bowl on HIGH (100%) power for 1 minute; stir. Microwave at additional 10- to 20-second intervals, stirring until smooth; cool.

COMBINE flour, baking soda and salt in small bowl. Beat butter, brown sugar, granulated sugar and vanilla extract in large mixer bowl. Beat in melted chocolate and egg. Gradually beat in flour mixture. Stir in peanuts. Drop by rounded tablespoon onto ungreased baking sheets.

BAKE in preheated 375°F. oven for 8 to 9 minutes or until edges are set but centers are still slightly soft. Let stand for 3 minutes; remove to wire racks to cool completely. Makes 2½ dozen cookies.

Pictured on pages 10 and 11.

chocolate
mint brownie cookies

1 1/2 cups (9 ounces) NESTLÉ® TOLL HOUSE®
     Semi-Sweet Chocolate Morsels, *divided*
1 3/4 cups all-purpose flour
  1/2 teaspoon baking soda
  1/4 teaspoon salt
  1/2 cup (1 stick) butter or margarine, softened
  1/2 cup granulated sugar
  1/4 cup packed brown sugar
   1 teaspoon vanilla extract
  1/2 teaspoon peppermint extract
   2 eggs
  3/4 cup chopped nuts

MELT *¾ cup* morsels in small, *heavy-duty* saucepan over *lowest possible* heat. When morsels begin to melt, remove from heat; stir. Return to heat for a few seconds at a time, stirring until smooth. Cool to room temperature.

COMBINE flour, baking soda and salt in small bowl. Beat butter, granulated sugar, brown sugar, vanilla extract and peppermint extract in large mixer bowl until creamy. Add eggs, one at a time, beating well after each addition. Beat in melted chocolate. Gradually beat in flour mixture. Stir in *remaining* morsels and nuts. Drop dough by rounded tablespoon onto ungreased baking sheets.

BAKE in preheated 350°F. oven for 8 to 12 minutes or until sides are set but centers are still soft. Let stand for 2 minutes; remove to wire racks to cool completely. Makes about 3 dozen cookies.

Pictured on page 15.

pumpkin orange cookies

2½ cups all-purpose flour
½ teaspoon baking soda
½ teaspoon salt
1 cup (2 sticks) butter or margarine
1 cup granulated sugar
½ cup packed brown sugar
1¼ cups LIBBY'S® Solid Pack Pumpkin
1 egg
2 tablespoons orange juice
1 teaspoon grated orange peel
½ cup chopped nuts (optional)
Orange Icing (recipe follows)

COMBINE flour, baking soda and salt in medium bowl. Beat butter, granulated sugar and brown sugar in large mixer bowl until creamy. Beat in pumpkin, egg, orange juice and orange peel until combined. Gradually beat in flour mixture. Stir in nuts.

DROP dough by rounded tablespoon onto ungreased baking sheets. Bake in preheated 375°F. oven for 12 to 14 minutes or until edges are set. Remove cookies immediately to wire rack to cool completely. Spread cookies with Orange Icing. Makes about 4 dozen cookies.

For Orange Icing:
COMBINE 1½ cups sifted powdered sugar, ½ teaspoon grated orange peel and enough orange juice until of desired consistency (1 to 3 tablespoons) in medium bowl. Stir until smooth.

Macadamia Nut White Chip Pumpkin Cookies (see recipe, page 14) and Pumpkin Orange Cookies (see recipe above)

crispy polynesian butterscotch cookies

1½ cups all-purpose flour
½ teaspoon baking soda
½ teaspoon salt
½ cup butter or margarine, softened
½ cup vegetable oil
½ cup granulated sugar
½ cup packed brown sugar
1 egg
1 teaspoon vanilla extract
1⅔ cups (11-ounce package) NESTLÉ® TOLL HOUSE®
   Butterscotch Morsels
½ cup quick oats
½ cup crushed cereal flakes
½ cup flaked coconut
½ cup chopped nuts

COMBINE flour, baking soda and salt in small bowl. Beat butter, oil, granulated sugar, brown sugar, egg and vanilla extract in large mixer bowl until creamy. Gradually beat in flour mixture. Stir in morsels, oats, crushed cereal, coconut and nuts. Drop by rounded tablespoon onto ungreased baking sheets.

BAKE in preheated 350°F. oven for 10 to 14 minutes or until edges are crisp but centers are still slightly soft. Let stand for 2 minutes; remove to wire racks to cool completely. Makes 3½ dozen cookies.

Pictured on page 26.

island cookies

1⅔ cups all-purpose flour
¾ teaspoon baking powder
½ teaspoon baking soda
½ teaspoon salt
¾ cup (1½ sticks) butter or margarine, softened
¾ cup packed brown sugar
⅓ cup granulated sugar
1 teaspoon vanilla extract
1 egg
2 cups (11½-ounce package) NESTLÉ® TOLL HOUSE®
    Milk Chocolate Morsels*
1 cup flaked coconut, toasted if desired
¾ cup macadamia nuts or walnuts, chopped

COMBINE flour, baking powder, baking soda and salt in small bowl. Beat butter, brown sugar, granulated sugar and vanilla extract in large mixer bowl until creamy. Beat in egg. Gradually beat in flour mixture. Stir in morsels, coconut and nuts. Drop by slightly rounded tablespoon onto ungreased baking sheets.

BAKE in preheated 375°F. oven for 8 to 11 minutes or until edges are lightly browned. Let stand for 2 minutes; remove to wire racks to cool completely. Makes about 3 dozen cookies.

*Note: NESTLÉ® TOLL HOUSE® Semi-Sweet Chocolate Morsels, Semi-Sweet Chocolate Mini-Morsels, Premier White Morsels or Butterscotch Morsels may be substituted for the Milk Chocolate Morsels.

oatmeal scotchies™

1¼ cups all-purpose flour
1 teaspoon baking soda
½ teaspoon salt
½ teaspoon ground cinnamon
1 cup (2 sticks) butter, softened
¾ cup granulated sugar
¾ cup packed brown sugar
2 eggs
1 teaspoon vanilla extract or grated orange peel
3 cups quick or old-fashioned oats
1⅔ cups (11-ounce package) NESTLÉ® TOLL HOUSE® Butterscotch Morsels

COMBINE flour, baking soda, salt and cinnamon in small bowl. Beat butter, granulated sugar, brown sugar, eggs and vanilla extract in large mixer bowl until creamy. Gradually beat in flour mixture. Stir in oats and morsels. Drop by rounded tablespoon onto ungreased baking sheets.

BAKE in preheated 375°F. oven for 7 to 8 minutes for chewy cookies or 9 to 10 minutes for crispy cookies. Let stand for 2 minutes; remove to wire racks to cool completely. Makes about 4 dozen cookies.

Bar Cookie Variation:
PREPARE dough as *above*. Spread dough into greased 15 x 10-inch jelly-roll pan. Bake in preheated 375°F. oven for 18 to 22 minutes or until very lightly browned. Cool completely in pan on rack. Makes 4 dozen.

Also pictured on the cover.

butterscotch apple cookies

2½ cups all-purpose flour

2 teaspoons ground cinnamon

1 teaspoon baking soda

½ teaspoon salt

1⅓ cups packed brown sugar

½ cup (1 stick) butter or margarine, softened

1 egg

½ cup apple juice

1⅔ cups (11-ounce package) NESTLÉ® TOLL HOUSE® Butterscotch Morsels, *divided*

¾ cup (1 small) unpeeled grated apple

¾ cup chopped walnuts, *divided*
Butterscotch Glaze (recipe follows)

COMBINE flour, cinnamon, baking soda and salt in medium bowl. Beat brown sugar and butter in large mixer bowl until creamy. Beat in egg. Gradually beat in flour mixture alternately with apple juice. Stir in *1½ cups* morsels, apple and *½ cup* walnuts. Drop by slightly rounded tablespoon onto lightly greased baking sheets.

BAKE in preheated 350°F. oven for 10 to 12 minutes or until lightly browned. Let stand for 2 minutes; remove to wire racks to cool completely. Spread with Butterscotch Glaze; sprinkle with *remaining* walnuts. Makes about 3½ dozen cookies.

For Butterscotch Glaze:
MELT *remaining* morsels and 2 tablespoons butter in small, *heavy-duty* saucepan over *lowest possible* heat. Remove from heat; stir in 1 cup sifted powdered sugar and 1 to 1½ tablespoons apple juice until smooth.

easy butterscotch chip cookies

1 package (18½ ounces) chocolate cake mix
½ cup vegetable oil
2 eggs
1⅔ cups (11-ounce package) NESTLÉ® TOLL HOUSE® Butterscotch Morsels
½ cup chopped pecans (optional)

COMBINE chocolate cake mix, oil and eggs in large bowl. Stir in morsels and pecans. Drop by rounded tablespoon onto ungreased baking sheets.

BAKE in preheated 350°F. oven for 8 to 10 minutes or until centers are just set. Let stand for 2 minutes; remove to wire racks to cool completely. Makes about 3½ dozen cookies.

Pictured on page 86.

Chopping Nuts

Keep a supply of chopped nuts on hand to add captivating flavor and texture to all kinds of cookies, cakes and other baked goods. Save time by chopping a large quantity of nuts at once and storing the extra in the freezer. To chop nuts quickly, place them on a cutting board and use a chef's knife to cut them into even-size pieces. Or, if you prefer, chop the nuts in your food processor, using several on-off turns to prevent chopping the nuts too finely. When time is short, look for chopped walnuts and pecans in the baking aisle of your supermarket.

white chip orange cookies

2 ¼ cups all-purpose flour
¾ teaspoon baking soda
½ teaspoon salt
1 cup butter or margarine, softened
½ cup granulated sugar
½ cup packed light brown sugar
1 egg
2 to 3 teaspoons grated orange peel
2 cups (12-ounce package) NESTLÉ® TOLL HOUSE® Premier White Morsels

COMBINE flour, baking soda and salt in small bowl. Beat butter, granulated sugar and brown sugar in large mixer bowl until creamy. Beat in egg and orange peel. Gradually beat in flour mixture. Stir in morsels. Drop dough by rounded tablespoon onto ungreased baking sheets.

BAKE in preheated 350°F. oven for 10 to 12 minutes or until edges are light golden brown. Let stand for 2 minutes; remove to wire racks to cool completely. Makes 39 cookies.

Also pictured on the cover.

White Chip Orange Cookies (see recipe above),
Double Chocolate Dream Cookies (see recipe, page 30) and
Crispy Polynesian Butterscotch Cookies (see recipe, page 20)

choc-oat-chip cookies

1¾ cups all-purpose flour
1 teaspoon baking soda
½ teaspoon salt (optional)
1¼ cups packed light brown sugar
1 cup (2 sticks) butter, softened
½ cup granulated sugar
2 eggs
2 tablespoons milk
2 teaspoons vanilla extract
2½ cups quick or old-fashioned oats
2 cups (12-ounce package) NESTLÉ® TOLL HOUSE® Semi-Sweet Chocolate Morsels
1 cup coarsely chopped nuts (optional)

COMBINE flour, baking soda and salt in small bowl. Beat brown sugar, butter and granulated sugar in large mixer bowl until creamy. Beat in eggs, milk and vanilla extract. Gradually beat in flour mixture. Stir in oats, morsels and nuts. Drop by rounded tablespoon onto ungreased baking sheets.

BAKE in preheated 375°F. oven for 9 to 10 minutes for chewy cookies or 12 to 13 minutes for crispy cookies. Let stand for 1 minute; remove to wire racks to cool completely. Makes about 4 dozen cookies.

Pictured on the cover and on page 34.

good-for-you
choc-oat-chip cookies

Lower Fat

1¾ cups all-purpose flour
1 teaspoon baking soda
½ teaspoon salt
½ teaspoon ground cinnamon
1¼ cups packed dark brown sugar
½ cup granulated sugar
½ cup (1 stick) margarine
½ cup unsweetened applesauce
2 egg whites
1 tablespoon vanilla extract
2½ cups quick or old-fashioned oats
2 cups (12-ounce package) NESTLÉ® TOLL HOUSE® Semi-Sweet Chocolate Morsels
½ cup chopped nuts

COMBINE flour, baking soda, salt and cinnamon in small bowl. Beat together brown sugar, granulated sugar, margarine and applesauce in large mixer bowl. Beat in egg whites and vanilla extract. Gradually beat in flour mixture. Stir in oats, morsels and nuts. Drop by rounded tablespoon onto greased baking sheets.

BAKE in preheated 375°F. oven for 9 to 10 minutes for chewy cookies or 12 to 13 minutes for crispy cookies. Let stand for 2 minutes; remove to wire racks to cool completely. Makes about 4 dozen cookies. About 120 calories and 5 grams fat per cookie.

double chocolate dream cookies

2¼ cups all-purpose flour
½ cup NESTLÉ® TOLL HOUSE® Baking Cocoa
1 teaspoon baking soda
½ teaspoon salt
1 cup butter or margarine, softened
1 cup packed brown sugar
¾ cup granulated sugar
1 teaspoon vanilla extract
2 eggs
2 cups (12-ounce package) NESTLÉ® TOLL HOUSE® Semi-Sweet Chocolate Morsels

COMBINE flour, cocoa, baking soda and salt in small bowl. Beat butter, brown sugar, granulated sugar and vanilla extract in mixer bowl until creamy. Beat in eggs about 2 minutes or until light and fluffy. Gradually beat in flour mixture. Stir in morsels. Drop by rounded tablespoon onto ungreased baking sheets.

BAKE in preheated 375°F. oven 8 to 10 minutes or until puffed. Let stand for 2 minutes; remove to wire racks to cool completely. Makes 4½ dozen cookies.

Pictured on the cover and on page 26.

The Best Cookies Ever

Here's a cookie jar-full of tips to help you turn out perfect cookies every time.

Baking sheets and pans of shiny, heavy-gauge aluminum bake cookies and bars more evenly than thin, dark metal or glass pans. Choose baking sheets that are the right size for your oven, allowing at least 2 inches of space between the sides of the baking sheet and the oven walls or door.

Grease baking sheets only when a recipe recommends it. Some cookies spread too much if the sheet is greased. When the recipe calls for ungreased baking sheets, cool and wash them between batches.

To prevent cookies from spreading too much on warm or humid days, spoon the cookie dough onto the baking sheets; chill the dough for a few minutes before baking.

For evenly shaped cookies, try a scoop. When a recipe calls for rounded tablespoons of dough, use a 1½-inch diameter scoop with dough leveled.

Butter and regular stick margarine work best for the recipes in this book (see Butter & Margarine, page 234). Also, all of the recipes were tested using large eggs.

To achieve the right oven temperature before baking, preheat your oven for about 10 minutes.

Bake cookies or brownies on the middle rack of the oven, one pan at a time, to prevent over-darkened bottoms and uncooked tops.

Check cookies and bars for doneness at the minimum baking time stated in the recipe. Remember, cookies continue to bake slightly after they are removed from the oven. For chewy cookies, take them out while they are still on the lighter side.

Let most cookies stand on the baking sheet for 1 or 2 minutes (or as long as directed in recipe) to continue cooking and to become firm enough to remove from the baking sheets. Then transfer cookies to wire racks.

sensibly delicious chocolate chip cookies

3 cups all-purpose flour
1½ teaspoons baking soda
1 teaspoon salt
1¼ cups packed dark brown sugar
½ cup granulated sugar
½ cup (1 stick) margarine, softened
1 teaspoon vanilla extract
2 egg whites
⅓ cup water
2 cups (12-ounce package) NESTLÉ® TOLL HOUSE® Semi-Sweet Chocolate Morsels
⅓ cup chopped nuts (optional)

COMBINE flour, baking soda and salt in medium bowl. Beat together brown sugar, granulated sugar, margarine and vanilla extract in large mixer bowl. Beat in egg whites. Gradually beat in flour mixture alternately with water. Stir in morsels and nuts. Drop by rounded tablespoon onto lightly greased baking sheets.

BAKE in preheated 350°F. oven for 10 to 12 minutes or until centers are set. Let stand for 2 minutes; remove to wire racks to cool completely. Makes about 5 dozen cookies. About 94 calories and 4 grams fat per cookie with nuts.

Sensibly Delicious Chocolate Chip Cookies (see recipe above),
Slimmer Chocolate Crinkle-Top Cookies (see recipe, page 63) and
Double Chocolate Chip Brownies (see recipe, page 49)

chunky chocolate chip peanut butter cookies

1¼ cups all-purpose flour
½ teaspoon baking soda
½ teaspoon salt
½ teaspoon ground cinnamon
¾ cup (1½ sticks) butter or margarine, softened
½ cup granulated sugar
½ cup packed brown sugar
½ cup creamy peanut butter
1 egg
1 teaspoon vanilla extract
2 cups (12-ounce package) NESTLÉ® TOLL HOUSE® Semi-Sweet Chocolate Morsels
½ cup coarsely chopped peanuts

COMBINE flour, baking soda, salt and cinnamon in small bowl. Beat butter, granulated sugar, brown sugar and peanut butter in large mixer bowl until creamy. Beat in egg and vanilla extract. Gradually beat in flour mixture. Stir in morsels and peanuts. Drop dough by rounded tablespoon onto ungreased baking sheets. Press down slightly to flatten into 2-inch circles.

BAKE in preheated 375°F. oven for 7 to 10 minutes or until edges are set but centers are still soft. Let stand for 4 minutes; remove to wire racks to cool completely. Makes about 3 dozen cookies.

Chunky Chocolate Chip Peanut Butter Cookies (see recipe above) and Choc-Oat-Chip Cookies (see recipe, page 28)

chocolate lover's cookies

ever since Mrs. Wakefield used
Nestlé Semi-Sweet Chocolate to invent the
Original Nestlé® Toll House® Cookie, the
Nestlé name has been synonymous with
chocolate. Bake new memories for your
family, choosing from this assortment of
decadent cookies from the Nestlé
Chocolate Hall of Fame. With goodies this
tasty, you'll have trouble keeping them
around for long!

*Chocolate Turtle Brownies (see recipe, page 38), Frosted
Double Chocolate Cookies (see recipe, page 55) and
Original Nestlé® Toll House® Chocolate Chip Cookies
(Bar Cookie Variation) (see recipe, page 9)*

chocolate turtle brownies

2 cups (12-ounce package) NESTLÉ® TOLL HOUSE®
Semi-Sweet Chocolate Morsels, *divided*

½ cup (1 stick) butter or margarine, cut into pieces

3 eggs

1¼ cups all-purpose flour

1 cup granulated sugar

1 teaspoon vanilla extract

¼ teaspoon baking soda

½ cup chopped walnuts

12 caramels, unwrapped

1 tablespoon milk

MELT *1 cup* morsels and butter in large, *heavy-duty* saucepan over *lowest possible* heat, stirring constantly until smooth. Remove from heat; stir in eggs. Add flour, granulated sugar, vanilla extract and baking soda; stir well. Spread batter into greased 13 x 9-inch baking pan; sprinkle with *remaining* morsels and walnuts.

BAKE in preheated 350°F. oven for 20 to 25 minutes or until wooden pick inserted in center comes out slightly sticky.

MICROWAVE caramels and milk in small, microwave-safe bowl on HIGH (100%) power for 1 minute; stir. Microwave at additional 10- to 20-second intervals, stirring until smooth. Drizzle over warm brownies. Cool completely in pan on wire rack. Cut into bars. Makes 2 dozen brownies.

Pictured on pages 36 and 37.

Melted Chocolate Magic

A touch of melted chocolate adds elegance to cookies, cakes, pies and candies, as well as many other desserts. Keep these decorating hints in mind the next time you want to dress up something sweet for your family or company. Start first by melting the chocolate (see Masterful Melting, page 234); use it to make one of these attractive trims.

Chocolate-Dipped Nuts: Dip large nuts halfway into melted chocolate; let excess chocolate drip off. For small nuts, use a small paintbrush to stroke on the chocolate. Place the nuts on waxed paper to dry.

Chocolate Leaves: Use nontoxic leaves, such as mint, lemon or strawberry leaves. With a small paint brush, add two or three coats of melted chocolate to the underside of each leaf. Wipe off any chocolate on the topside of the leaf. Allow the chocolate to set up between coats. Place the leaves, chocolate sides up, on a waxed-paper-lined baking sheet; chill until hardened. Before using, peel the leaf away from the chocolate.

Chocolate Designs: Place slightly cooled, melted chocolate in a heavy-duty plastic bag. Cut a small hole in the corner of the bag. Drizzle heart shapes or other designs onto waxed paper. Chill until firm.

Chocolate Cutouts: Melt 1 cup (6 ounces) of NESTLÉ® TOLL HOUSE® Semi-Sweet Chocolate Morsels or 1 cup (6 ounces) NESTLÉ® TOLL HOUSE® Premier White Morsels with 1 tablespoon shortening; cool slightly. Pour the chocolate mixture onto a waxed paper-lined baking sheet, spreading it ⅛- to ¼-inch thick. Chill the chocolate until almost set. Firmly press hors d'oeuvre or small cookie cutters into the chocolate. Chill. Before serving, lift the cutouts from the baking sheet.

Chocolate-Dipped Fruit: Melt 1 cup (6 ounces) of NESTLÉ® TOLL HOUSE® Semi-Sweet Chocolate Morsels or 1 cup (6 ounces) NESTLÉ® TOLL HOUSE® Premier White Morsels with 2 tablespoons shortening. Dip fruit into chocolate mixture; shake off excess. Place on waxed paper-lined baking sheet; chill until firm.

german chocolate brownies

- 1 package (18½ ounces) chocolate cake mix
- 1 cup chopped nuts
- ½ cup (1 stick) butter or margarine, melted
- 1 cup NESTLÉ® CARNATION® Evaporated Milk, *divided*
- 35 (10-ounce package) caramels, unwrapped
- 2 cups (12-ounce package) NESTLÉ® TOLL HOUSE® Semi-Sweet Chocolate Morsels

COMBINE cake mix and nuts in large bowl. Stir in butter. Stir in ⅔ *cup* evaporated milk (batter will be thick). Spread *half* of batter into ungreased 13 x 9-inch baking pan. Bake in preheated 350°F. oven for 15 minutes.

COOK caramels and *remaining* evaporated milk in small saucepan over low heat, stirring constantly until caramels are melted. Sprinkle morsels over hot base; drizzle with caramel mixture.

DROP *remaining* batter by heaping teaspoon over caramel mixture. Bake at 350°F. for 25 to 30 minutes or until center is set. Cool completely in pan on wire rack. Cut into bars. Makes 4 dozen.

double espresso brownies

ESPRESSO BROWNIES
- 1 cup all-purpose flour
- ½ teaspoon baking powder
- ¼ teaspoon salt
- ⅓ cup hot water
- 1 tablespoon instant espresso powder or instant coffee crystals
- 1 cup granulated sugar
- ½ cup (1 stick) butter or margarine
- 2 cups (12-ounce package) NESTLÉ® TOLL HOUSE® Semi-Sweet Chocolate Morsels, *divided*
- 3 eggs

ESPRESSO FROSTING
- ½ cup whipping cream
- 1 teaspoon instant espresso powder or instant coffee crystals
- ½ cup sifted powdered sugar

For Espresso Brownies:

COMBINE flour, baking powder and salt in small bowl. Heat water and espresso in medium saucepan over low heat, stirring to dissolve espresso. Add granulated sugar and butter; cook, stirring constantly, until mixture comes to a boil. Remove from heat; stir in *1 cup* morsels until smooth. Add eggs, one at a time, stirring well after each addition. Stir in flour mixture. Pour into greased 9-inch square baking pan.

BAKE in preheated 350°F. oven for 25 to 30 minutes or until wooden pick inserted in center comes out slightly sticky. Cool completely in pan on wire rack.

For Espresso Frosting:

HEAT cream and espresso in small, *heavy-duty* saucepan over low heat, stirring to dissolve espresso. Add *remaining* morsels, stirring until smooth. Remove from heat; stir in powdered sugar. Chill until frosting is of spreading consistency. Spread onto brownies. Cut into squares. Makes 3 dozen brownies.

craggy-topped fudge brownies

1 cup granulated sugar
½ cup (1 stick) butter or margarine
2 cups (12-ounce package) NESTLÉ® TOLL HOUSE®
   Semi-Sweet Chocolate Morsels, *divided*
3 eggs
1⅓ cups all-purpose flour
1 teaspoon vanilla extract
¼ teaspoon baking soda
⅓ cup chopped nuts

HEAT granulated sugar and butter in medium saucepan over low heat, stirring until butter is melted. Remove from heat. Add 1¼ *cups* morsels; stir until melted. Stir in eggs. Stir in flour, vanilla extract and baking soda until combined. Spread into greased 13 x 9-inch baking pan.

BAKE in preheated 350°F. oven for 18 to 22 minutes or until wooden pick inserted in center comes out slightly sticky.

SPRINKLE with *remaining* morsels and nuts while still hot. Cover with foil; chill in pan until completely cooled. Cut into bars. Makes 2 dozen brownies.

Pictured on page 44.

moist brownies

BROWNIES

1 ¼ cups all-purpose flour

½ teaspoon baking soda

¼ teaspoon salt

¾ cup granulated sugar

½ cup (1 stick) butter or margarine

2 tablespoons water

1 ½ cups (9 ounces) NESTLÉ® TOLL HOUSE® Semi-Sweet Chocolate Morsels, *divided*

1 teaspoon vanilla extract

2 eggs

FROSTING

1 container (16 ounces) prepared vanilla frosting

1 tube (4 ¼ ounces) chocolate decorating icing

For Brownies:

COMBINE flour, baking soda and salt in small bowl. Combine sugar, butter and water in medium saucepan. Bring *just to a boil* over medium heat, stirring constantly; remove from heat. (Or, combine granulated sugar, butter and water in medium, microwave-safe bowl. Microwave on HIGH [100%] power for 3 minutes, stirring halfway through cooking time. Stir until smooth.)

ADD *1 cup* morsels and vanilla extract; stir until smooth. Add eggs, one at a time, stirring well after each addition. Stir in flour mixture and *remaining* morsels. Spread into greased 9-inch square baking pan.

BAKE in preheated 350°F. oven for 20 to 30 minutes or until center is set. Cool completely (center will sink) in pan on rack.

For Frosting:

SPREAD vanilla frosting over brownies. Squeeze chocolate icing in parallel lines over frosting. Drag wooden pick through chocolate icing to feather. Let stand until frosting is set. Cut into bars. Makes 16 brownies.

Pictured on page 44.

chocolate macaroon bars

1 package (18¼ ounces) chocolate cake mix
⅓ cup butter or margarine, softened
2 eggs, *divided*
1¼ cups (14-ounce can) NESTLÉ® CARNATION® Sweetened
    Condensed Milk
1 teaspoon vanilla extract
2 cups (12-ounce package) NESTLÉ® TOLL HOUSE®
    Semi-Sweet Chocolate Morsels
1⅓ cups flaked coconut, *divided*
¾ cup chopped nuts (optional)

BEAT cake mix, butter and *1 egg* in large mixer bowl until mixture
is crumbly. Firmly press mixture onto bottom of greased 13 x 9-inch
baking pan.

COMBINE sweetened condensed milk, *remaining* egg and
vanilla extract in medium bowl; stir in morsels, *1 cup* coconut
and nuts. Spread over mixture in baking pan. Sprinkle with
remaining coconut.

BAKE in preheated 350°F. oven for 30 to 40 minutes or until
golden brown (center will set when cooled). Cool completely in
pan on wire rack. Cut into bars. Makes 2½ dozen bars.

Craggy-Topped Fudge Brownies (see recipe, page 42),
Chocolate Macaroon Bars (see recipe above) and
Moist Brownies (see recipe, page 43)

triple chocolate cookies

1¾ cups all-purpose flour
½ cup NESTLÉ® TOLL HOUSE® Baking Cocoa
1 teaspoon baking soda
2 cups (12-ounce package) NESTLÉ® TOLL HOUSE®
   Semi-Sweet Chocolate Morsels, *divided*
⅓ cup butter or margarine, cut into pieces
1¼ cups (14-ounce can) NESTLÉ® CARNATION® Sweetened
   Condensed Milk
1 egg
1 teaspoon vanilla extract
½ cup chopped nuts

COMBINE flour, cocoa and baking soda in medium bowl. Melt *1 cup* morsels and butter in large, *heavy-duty* saucepan over *lowest possible* heat, stirring until smooth. Remove from heat. Stir in sweetened condensed milk, egg and vanilla extract; mix well. Stir in flour mixture. Stir in nuts and *remaining* morsels (dough will be soft). Drop dough by rounded tablespoon onto lightly greased baking sheets.

BAKE in preheated 350°F. oven for 8 to 10 minutes or until edges are set but centers are still slightly soft. Let stand for 2 minutes; remove to wire racks to cool completely. Makes about 3½ dozen cookies.

chocolate fudge brownies

1⅔ cups granulated sugar

½ cup (1 stick) butter or margarine

2 tablespoons water

2 bars (2 ounces *each*) NESTLÉ® TOLL HOUSE® Unsweetened Baking Chocolate, broken into pieces

2 eggs

1½ teaspoons vanilla extract

1⅓ cups all-purpose flour

¼ teaspoon baking soda

¼ teaspoon salt

½ cup chopped nuts (optional)

MICROWAVE granulated sugar, butter and water in large, microwave-safe bowl on HIGH (100%) power for 4 to 5 minutes or until mixture bubbles, stirring once. (Or, heat granulated sugar, butter and water in medium saucepan just to boiling, stirring constantly. Remove from heat.) Add baking bars, stirring until melted.

STIR in eggs, one at a time, beating well after each addition. Stir in vanilla extract. Gradually stir in flour, baking soda and salt. Stir in nuts. Pour into greased 13 x 9-inch baking pan.

BAKE in preheated 350°F. oven for 15 to 20 minutes or until wooden pick inserted in center comes out slightly sticky. Cool completely in pan on wire rack. Cut into bars. Makes 2 dozen brownies.

Peanut Butter Brownie Variation:
PREPARE batter as *above* without nuts; *do not pour into pan.* Combine ½ cup creamy or chunky peanut butter, 3 tablespoons granulated sugar and 2 tablespoons milk in medium, microwave-safe bowl. Microwave on HIGH (100%) power for 45 seconds; stir until smooth. Pour batter into pan. Spoon peanut butter mixture over top; swirl with spoon. Bake in preheated 350°F. oven for 20 to 25 minutes. Cool completely in pan on wire rack. Cut into bars. Makes 2 dozen brownies.

black forest brownie squares

2 cups (12-ounce package) NESTLÉ® TOLL HOUSE®
Semi-Sweet Chocolate Morsels, *divided*

½ cup butter or margarine, cut into pieces

3 eggs

1¼ cups all-purpose flour

1 cup granulated sugar

1 teaspoon vanilla extract

¼ teaspoon baking soda

1½ cups frozen whipped topping, thawed

2 cups (21-ounce can) cherry pie filling or topping

MELT *1 cup* morsels and butter in large, *heavy-duty* saucepan over *lowest possible* heat, stirring until smooth. Remove from heat; stir in eggs. Gradually stir in flour, granulated sugar, vanilla extract and baking soda. Stir in *remaining* morsels. Spread into greased 13 x 9-inch baking pan.

BAKE in preheated 350°F. oven for 20 to 25 minutes or until wooden pick inserted in center comes out slightly sticky. Cool completely in pan on wire rack. Spread with whipped topping. Top with pie filling. Cut into squares. Makes 24 squares.

Pictured on pages 66 and 67.

Save Some for Later

If cookies disappear in a hurry at your house, tuck some away for another time. For best results, cool the cookies completely before storing. Place the cookies in tightly covered containers or plastic bags. This way the humidity won't soften crisp cookies and the air won't dry out soft ones. Don't pack crisp and soft cookies in the same container. You can keep most cookies at room temperature for up to three days. For longer storage, store the cookies in freezer bags or containers and freeze them for up to 12 months. Thaw cookies about 15 minutes before serving.

double chocolate chip brownies

Lower Fat

2 cups (12-ounce package) NESTLÉ® TOLL HOUSE®
Semi-Sweet Chocolate Morsels, *divided*
1 cup granulated sugar
½ cup unsweetened applesauce
2 tablespoons margarine
3 egg whites
1¼ cups all-purpose flour
¼ teaspoon baking soda
¼ teaspoon salt
1 teaspoon vanilla extract
¼ cup chopped nuts (optional)

HEAT *1 cup* morsels, granulated sugar, applesauce and margarine in large, *heavy-duty* saucepan over low heat; stir until smooth. Remove from heat. Cool slightly. Stir in egg whites. Combine flour, baking soda and salt. Stir into chocolate mixture. Stir in vanilla extract. Stir in *remaining* morsels and nuts. Spread into greased 13 x 9-inch baking pan.

BAKE in preheated 350°F. oven 16 to 20 minutes or just until set. Cool completely in pan on wire rack. Cut into bars. Makes 2 dozen. About 159 calories and 7 grams fat per brownie with nuts.

Pictured on page 32.

white chip chocolate cookies

2¼ cups all-purpose flour
⅔ cup NESTLÉ® TOLL HOUSE® Baking Cocoa
1 teaspoon baking soda
¼ teaspoon salt
1 cup (2 sticks) butter or margarine, softened
¾ cup granulated sugar
⅔ cup packed brown sugar
1 teaspoon vanilla extract
2 eggs
2 cups (12-ounce package) NESTLÉ® TOLL HOUSE® Premier White Morsels

COMBINE flour, cocoa, baking soda and salt in small bowl. Beat butter, granulated sugar, brown sugar and vanilla extract in large mixer bowl until creamy. Beat in eggs, one at a time, beating well after each addition. Gradually beat in flour mixture. Stir in morsels. Drop by well-rounded teaspoon onto ungreased baking sheets.

BAKE in preheated 350°F. oven for 9 to 11 minutes or until centers are set. Let stand for 2 minutes; remove to wire racks to cool completely. Makes about 5 dozen cookies.

chocolate lover's cookies

double chocolate peanut butter thumbprint cookies

1½ cups all-purpose flour
⅓ cup NESTLÉ® TOLL HOUSE® Baking Cocoa
1½ teaspoons baking powder
¼ teaspoon salt
2 cups (12-ounce package) NESTLÉ® TOLL HOUSE® Semi-Sweet Chocolate Morsels, *divided*
1 cup granulated sugar
About 1 cup chunky or creamy peanut butter (not all-natural), *divided*
⅓ cup butter or margarine, softened
1½ teaspoons vanilla extract
2 eggs

COMBINE flour, cocoa, baking powder and salt in small bowl. Melt *1 cup* morsels in small, *heavy-duty* saucepan over *lowest possible* heat, stirring constantly until smooth.

BEAT granulated sugar, *⅓ cup* peanut butter, butter and vanilla extract in large mixer bowl until creamy. Beat in melted chocolate. Add eggs, one at a time, beating well after each addition. Gradually beat in flour mixture. Stir in *remaining* morsels. Cover; chill just until firm.

SHAPE dough into 1½-inch balls. Place balls on ungreased baking sheets. Press ½-inch deep centers with thumb. Fill each center with about ½ *teaspoon* peanut butter.

BAKE in preheated 350°F. oven for 10 to 15 minutes or until sides are set but centers are still slightly soft. Let stand for 2 minutes; remove to wire racks to cool completely. Makes about 3½ dozen.

chocolate amaretto bars

CRUST
- 3 cups all-purpose flour
- 1 cup (2 sticks) butter or margarine, cut into pieces and softened
- ½ cup packed brown sugar

FILLING
- 4 eggs
- ¾ cup light corn syrup
- ¾ cup granulated sugar
- ¼ cup amaretto liqueur or ½ teaspoon almond extract
- 2 tablespoons butter or margarine, melted
- 1 tablespoon cornstarch
- 2 cups (about 7 ounces) sliced almonds
- 2 cups (12-ounce package) NESTLÉ® TOLL HOUSE® Semi-Sweet Chocolate Morsels, *divided*

Chocolate Drizzle (optional recipe follows)

For Crust:
BEAT flour, butter and brown sugar in large mixer bowl until crumbly. Press into greased 13 x 9-inch baking pan. Bake in preheated 350°F. oven 12 to 15 minutes or until golden brown.

For Filling:
BEAT eggs, corn syrup, granulated sugar, liqueur, butter and cornstarch in medium bowl with wire whisk. Stir in almonds and 1⅔ *cups* morsels. Pour and spread over hot crust.

BAKE at 350°F. for 25 to 30 minutes or until center is set. Cool in pan to room temperature on wire rack. If desired, top with Chocolate Drizzle. Chill for 5 minutes or until chocolate is firm. Cut into bars. Makes 2½ dozen bars.

For Chocolate Drizzle:
PLACE *remaining* morsels in heavy-duty plastic bag. Microwave on HIGH (100%) power for 45 seconds; knead bag to mix. Microwave at additional 10-second intervals, kneading until smooth. Cut a small hole in corner of bag; squeeze to drizzle chocolate over bars.

frosted brownies

BROWNIES
- ⅔ cup all-purpose flour
- ½ teaspoon baking powder
- ¼ teaspoon salt
- 1 cup granulated sugar
- ½ cup (1 stick) butter or margarine, softened
- 2 eggs
- 3 envelopes (1 ounce *each*) NESTLÉ® TOLL HOUSE® CHOCO BAKE® Unsweetened Chocolate Flavor
- 1 teaspoon vanilla extract
- ½ cup chopped nuts

FUDGE FROSTING
- 3 tablespoons butter or margarine, softened
- 1 envelope (1 ounce) NESTLÉ® TOLL HOUSE® CHOCO BAKE® Unsweetened Chocolate Flavor
- 2 teaspoons milk
- ½ teaspoon vanilla extract
- 1 cup sifted powdered sugar

For Brownies:
COMBINE flour, baking powder and salt in small bowl. Beat granulated sugar, butter, eggs, Choco Bake and vanilla extract in small mixer bowl until creamy. Gradually beat in flour mixture. Stir in nuts. Spread into greased 8-inch square baking pan.

BAKE in preheated 350°F. oven for 25 to 30 minutes or until wooden pick inserted in center comes out slightly sticky. Cool brownies completely in pan on wire rack.

For Fudge Frosting:
BEAT butter, Choco Bake, milk and vanilla extract in small mixer bowl until well blended. Gradually beat in powdered sugar until creamy. Spread onto brownies. Cut into bars. Makes 16 brownies.

frosted double chocolate cookies

2 cups (12-ounce package) NESTLÉ® TOLL HOUSE®
  Semi-Sweet Chocolate Morsels, *divided*
1¼ cups all-purpose flour
¾ teaspoon baking soda
½ teaspoon salt
½ cup (1 stick) butter or margarine, softened
½ cup packed brown sugar
¼ cup granulated sugar
1 teaspoon vanilla extract
1 egg
½ cup chopped nuts (optional)
  Chocolate Frosting (recipe follows)

MICROWAVE *¾ cup* morsels in small, microwave-safe bowl on HIGH (100%) power for 1 minute; stir. Microwave at additional 10- to 20-second intervals, stirring until smooth; cool to room temperature.

COMBINE flour, baking soda and salt in small bowl. Beat butter, brown sugar, granulated sugar and vanilla extract in large mixer bowl until creamy. Beat in melted chocolate and egg. Gradually beat in flour mixture. Stir in *¾ cup* morsels and nuts. Drop by rounded tablespoon onto ungreased baking sheets.

BAKE in preheated 375°F. oven for 8 to 9 minutes or until edges are set but centers are still slightly soft. Let stand for 3 minutes; remove to wire racks to cool completely. Spread Chocolate Frosting on cookies. Makes about 2½ dozen cookies.

For Chocolate Frosting:
MICROWAVE *remaining ½ cup* morsels and 2 tablespoons butter or margarine in medium, microwave-safe bowl on HIGH (100%) power for 30 seconds; stir. Microwave at additional 10- to 20-second intervals, stirring until smooth. Add 1¼ cups sifted powdered sugar and 2 tablespoons milk; stir until smooth.

Pictured on pages 36 and 37.

chocolate peanut buddy bars

1 cup creamy or chunky peanut butter
6 tablespoons butter or margarine, softened
1¼ cups granulated sugar
3 eggs
1 teaspoon vanilla extract
1 cup all-purpose flour
¼ teaspoon salt
2 cups (11½-ounce package) NESTLÉ® TOLL HOUSE® Milk
   Chocolate Morsels, *divided*

BEAT peanut butter and butter in large mixer bowl until smooth. Beat in sugar, eggs and vanilla extract. Beat in flour and salt. Stir in *1 cup* morsels. Spread into ungreased 13 x 9-inch pan.

BAKE in preheated 350°F. oven for 25 to 30 minutes or until edges are lightly browned. Immediately sprinkle with *remaining* morsels. Let stand for 5 minutes or until morsels are shiny and soft; spread evenly. Cool completely in pan on wire rack. Cut into bars. Makes 3 dozen bars.

Cookie Decorating Tips

Put on your artist's cap and use cookies as your canvas. These designer tips will help you get started.

Always cool baked cookies before decorating with icing and candies.

For colored frosting, tint vanilla frosting with food coloring. Use liquid coloring for pastel colors. Use paste food coloring for more vibrant colors, starting with a small amount, then adding more as needed.

To pipe frosting on cookies, use a pastry bag with tips, purchased frosting in tubes or a plastic bag with a corner snipped off. If spreading frosting with a knife, thin the frosting with milk to desired consistency.

Top cookies with candy sprinkles, cinnamon red hots, chopped nuts, NESTLÉ® TOLL HOUSE® Morsels, raisins, candy corn, licorice or coconut.

chocolate cookie turtle shapes

2 cups (120) pecan halves
1 package (18 ounces) refrigerated NESTLÉ® TOLL HOUSE®
   Chocolate Chip Cookie Dough
20 caramels, unwrapped
2 tablespoons milk

SOAK pecans in water for 5 minutes. Arrange 5 pecans on ungreased baking sheet (1 for head, 4 for legs), leaving about a 1-inch circle in center.

SHAPE level tablespoon of cookie dough into ball; place over circle, pressing onto pecans. Repeat with remaining pecans and dough, placing turtles 2 inches apart on ungreased baking sheets.

BAKE in preheated 350°F. oven for 11 to 13 minutes or until edges are crisp. Let stand for 1 minute; remove to wire racks to cool completely.

MICROWAVE caramels and milk in microwave-safe bowl on HIGH (100%) power for 1½ minutes; stir. Microwave at additional 10-second intervals until melted. Drizzle over turtles. Makes about 2 dozen cookies.

Cookie Care-Packages

When you plan to mail cookies, choose a recipe for firm cookies, avoiding soft, brittle or delicate varieties. Drop cookies, slice-and-bake cookies and uncut bar cookies travel best. Avoid frosted cookies because they may stick to each other or to the packaging. After baking, cool the cookies completely; wrap two at a time, back to back in plastic wrap. Stack cookies snugly, on end, in a sturdy box, using a filler such as bubble wrap, foam packing pieces or crumpled waxed paper or paper towels to fill in extra spaces. Seal, label and mail.

chocolate oatmeal bars

  1 cup all-purpose flour
  ½ teaspoon ground cinnamon
  1 cup (2 sticks) butter or margarine, softened
  ½ cup granulated sugar
  ½ cup packed brown sugar
1½ teaspoons vanilla extract
  1 egg
1¼ cups quick or old-fashioned oats
  2 cups (11½-ounce package) NESTLÉ® TOLL HOUSE® Milk Chocolate Morsels, *divided*
  ¾ cup finely chopped walnuts, *divided*

COMBINE flour and cinnamon in small bowl. Beat butter, granulated sugar, brown sugar and vanilla extract in large mixer bowl until creamy. Beat in egg. Gradually beat in flour mixture. Stir in oats, *¾ cup* morsels and *½ cup* walnuts. Spread into lightly greased 13 x 9-inch baking pan.

BAKE in preheated 350°F. oven for 22 to 28 minutes or until center is set. Immediately sprinkle with *remaining* morsels; let stand for 5 minutes or until morsels are shiny. Spread morsels; sprinkle with *remaining* nuts. Cool completely in pan on wire rack. Cut into bars. Makes 2½ dozen bars.

chewy cocoa brownies

1⅔ cups granulated sugar
¾ cup butter or margarine, melted
2 tablespoons water
2 eggs
2 teaspoons vanilla extract
1⅓ cups all-purpose flour
¾ cup NESTLÉ® TOLL HOUSE® Baking Cocoa
½ teaspoon baking powder
¼ teaspoon salt
¾ cup chopped nuts (optional)
Sifted powdered sugar

STIR together granulated sugar, butter and water in large bowl. Stir in eggs and vanilla extract. Combine flour, cocoa, baking powder and salt in medium bowl; stir into sugar mixture. Stir in nuts. Spread into greased 13 x 9-inch baking pan.

BAKE in preheated 350°F. oven for 18 to 25 minutes or until wooden pick inserted in center comes out slightly sticky. Cool completely in pan on wire rack. Sprinkle with powdered sugar. Cut into bars. Makes 2 dozen brownies.

Pictured on page 86.

Sift on a Sugar Stencil

Transform everyday cookies or bars into special ones by decorating the tops with a powdered sugar stencil. To make the stencil, cut a piece of waxed paper the same size as the cookies or bars. In the center of the waxed paper, draw a shape, tracing the design or using a tiny cookie or hors d'oeuvre cutter as a pattern. Using scissors, cut out the center shape. (If you prefer, look for small stencils in craft stores rather than making your own.) Decorate the cookies or bars by placing the stencil over each and sifting powdered sugar over the stencil. Then, remove the stencil carefully.

chocolate lover's cookies

marbled chocolate brownies

1⅓ cups all-purpose flour
⅓ cup NESTLÉ® TOLL HOUSE® Baking Cocoa
¼ teaspoon baking soda
¼ teaspoon salt
1¼ cups granulated sugar
1 cup (6 ounces) NESTLÉ® TOLL HOUSE® Semi-Sweet
   Chocolate Morsels
½ cup unsweetened applesauce
2 tablespoons margarine
3 egg whites
1 teaspoon vanilla extract
4 ounces light cream cheese (Neufchâtel), softened
1 tablespoon granulated sugar
1 tablespoon nonfat milk

COMBINE flour, cocoa, baking soda and salt in small bowl. Heat
1¼ cups granulated sugar, morsels, applesauce and margarine in a
large, *heavy-duty* saucepan over low heat, stirring constantly just
until morsels are melted. Remove from heat. Cool slightly. Stir in
egg whites. Add flour mixture and vanilla extract; stir well. Spread
into a greased 13 x 9-inch baking pan.

STIR together cream cheese, 1 tablespoon granulated sugar and
milk in small bowl. Drop by rounded teaspoon over batter; swirl
over surface of batter with back of spoon.

BAKE in preheated 325°F. oven for 22 to 28 minutes or just
until set. Cool completely in pan on wire rack. Cut into bars.
Makes 2¼ dozen brownies. About 110 calories and 3 grams
fat per brownie.

deep chocolate cheesecake bars

CRUST

1½ cups all-purpose flour

½ cup packed brown sugar

½ cup (1 stick) butter or margarine, melted

CHEESECAKE TOPPING

2 cups (12-ounce package) NESTLÉ® TOLL HOUSE®
Semi-Sweet Chocolate Morsels

2 packages (8 ounces *each*) cream cheese, softened

⅔ cup granulated sugar

2 teaspoons vanilla extract

2 eggs

½ cup NESTLÉ® CARNATION® Evaporated Milk
Sifted powdered sugar

For Crust:
COMBINE flour, brown sugar and butter in medium bowl; press onto bottom of greased 13 x 9-inch baking pan. Bake in preheated 350°F. oven for 10 to 12 minutes or until golden brown around edges.

For Cheesecake Topping:
MICROWAVE morsels in medium, microwave-safe bowl on HIGH (100%) power for 1 minute; stir. Microwave at additional 10- to 20-second intervals, stirring until smooth. Cool to room temperature. Beat cream cheese, granulated sugar and vanilla extract in medium mixer bowl until smooth. Beat in eggs. Gradually beat in evaporated milk and melted chocolate. Pour over crust.

BAKE in 350°F. oven for 25 to 35 minutes or until center is set. Cool in pan to room temperature on wire rack; chill until firm. Sprinkle with powdered sugar. Cut into diamonds (see Creative Cuts tip box, *page 74*) or bars. Makes 4 dozen bars.

slimmer chocolate crinkle-top cookies

Lower Fat

2 cups (12-ounce package) NESTLÉ® TOLL HOUSE®
  Semi-Sweet Chocolate Morsels, *divided*

1½ cups all-purpose flour

1½ teaspoons baking powder

¼ teaspoon salt

1 cup granulated sugar

2 tablespoons margarine, softened

1½ teaspoons vanilla extract

2 egg whites

¼ cup water

½ cup powdered sugar

MELT *1 cup* morsels in small, *heavy-duty* saucepan over *lowest possible* heat. When morsels begin to melt, remove from heat; stir. Return to heat for a few seconds at a time, stirring until smooth. Cool to room temperature.

COMBINE flour, baking powder and salt in small bowl. Beat together granulated sugar, margarine and vanilla extract in large mixer bowl. Beat in melted chocolate; beat in egg whites. Gradually beat in flour mixture alternately with water. Stir in *remaining* morsels. Cover; chill until firm.

SHAPE dough into 1½-inch balls; roll in powdered sugar to coat generously. Place on greased baking sheets.

BAKE in preheated 350°F. oven for 10 to 15 minutes or until sides are set but centers are still slightly soft. Cool for 2 minutes; remove to wire racks to cool completely. Makes about 3 dozen cookies. About 100 calories and 4 grams fat per cookie.

Pictured on page 32.

white chip brownies

1 cup all-purpose flour
½ cup NESTLÉ® TOLL HOUSE® Baking Cocoa
¾ teaspoon baking powder
¼ teaspoon salt
1¼ cups granulated sugar
¾ cup (1½ sticks) butter or margarine, melted
2 teaspoons vanilla extract
3 eggs
2 cups (12-ounce package) NESTLÉ® TOLL HOUSE® Premier White Morsels, *divided*

COMBINE flour, cocoa, baking powder and salt in medium bowl. Beat granulated sugar, butter and vanilla extract together in large mixer bowl until creamy. Add eggs, one at a time, beating well after each addition. Gradually beat in flour mixture. Stir in *1½ cups* morsels. Pour into greased 9-inch square baking pan.

BAKE in preheated 350°F. oven for 25 to 30 minutes or until wooden pick inserted in center comes out slightly sticky. Cool completely (center will sink) in pan on wire rack.

PLACE *remaining* morsels in heavy-duty plastic bag. Microwave on MEDIUM-HIGH (70%) power for 45 seconds; knead bag to mix. Microwave at additional 10- to 20-second intervals, kneading until smooth. Cut a small hole in corner of bag; squeeze to drizzle over brownies. Chill for 5 minutes or until drizzle is firm. Cut into bars. Makes 16 brownies.

Pictured on page 82.

fudgy caramel brownies

2 cups (11½-ounce package) NESTLÉ® TOLL HOUSE® Semi-Sweet Chocolate Mega Morsels, *divided*

½ cup (1 stick) butter or margarine, cut into pieces

3 eggs

1¼ cups all-purpose flour

1 cup granulated sugar

1 teaspoon vanilla extract

¼ teaspoon baking soda

½ cup chopped nuts

12 caramels, unwrapped

1 tablespoon milk

MELT *1 cup* morsels and butter in large, *heavy-duty* saucepan over *lowest possible* heat. When morsels begin to melt, remove from heat; stir. Return to heat for a few seconds at a time, stirring until smooth. Remove from heat; stir in eggs. Add flour, sugar, vanilla extract and baking soda; stir well. Spread batter into greased 13 x 9-inch baking pan; sprinkle with *remaining* morsels and nuts.

BAKE in preheated 350°F. oven for 20 to 25 minutes or until wooden pick inserted in center comes out slightly sticky.

MICROWAVE caramels and milk in small, microwave-safe bowl on HIGH (100%) power for 1 minute; stir. Microwave at additional 10- to 20-second intervals, stirring until smooth. Drizzle over warm brownies. Cool completely in pan on wire rack. Makes 2 dozen brownies.

bar cookies galore

for afternoon snacktimes, potluck gatherings or any occasion, bar cookies and brownies are popular. Make each of these rich recipes from everyday ingredients and you'll have plenty of time to enjoy the scrumptious results. Treat loved ones to this medley of tried-and-true goodies.

Butterscotch Cream Cheese Bars (see recipe, page 68),
Chocolate Peanut Butter Bars (see recipe, page 69) and
Black Forest Brownie Squares (see recipe, page 48)

butterscotch
cream cheese bars

1⅔ cups (11-ounce package) NESTLÉ® TOLL HOUSE®
    Butterscotch Morsels
6 tablespoons (¾ stick) butter or margarine
2 cups graham cracker crumbs
2 cups chopped walnuts
2 packages (8 ounces *each*) cream cheese, softened
½ cup granulated sugar
4 eggs
¼ cup all-purpose flour
2 tablespoons lemon juice

MELT morsels and butter in medium, *heavy-duty* saucepan over *lowest possible* heat, stirring constantly until smooth. Stir in crumbs and walnuts. Reserve *2 cups* crumb mixture for topping; press *remaining* mixture into ungreased 15 x 10-inch jelly-roll pan. Bake in preheated 350°F. oven for 12 minutes.

BEAT cream cheese and granulated sugar in large mixer bowl until creamy. Add eggs, one at a time, beating well after each addition. Gradually beat in flour and lemon juice. Pour over crust; sprinkle with reserved crumb mixture.

BAKE at 350°F. for 20 to 25 minutes or until set. Cool completely in pan on wire rack. Cut into diamonds (see Creative Cuts tip box, *page 74*) or bars; chill. Makes 4 dozen bars.

Pictured on pages 66 and 67.

chocolate peanut butter bars

1¾ cups all-purpose flour

½ teaspoon baking soda

1¼ cups granulated sugar

¾ cup creamy or chunky peanut butter

½ cup butter or margarine, softened

1 teaspoon vanilla extract

1 egg

2 cups (12-ounce package) NESTLÉ® TOLL HOUSE®
Semi-Sweet Chocolate Morsels, *divided*

COMBINE flour and baking soda in small bowl. Beat granulated sugar, peanut butter, butter and vanilla extract in large mixer bowl until creamy. Beat in egg. Gradually beat in flour mixture. Stir in *1¼ cups* morsels. Press into ungreased 13 x 9-inch baking pan. Sprinkle with *remaining* morsels; press down slightly.

BAKE in preheated 350°F. oven for 20 to 25 minutes or until center is set. Cool completely in pan on wire rack. Chill for a few minutes. Cut into bars. Makes 3 dozen bars.

Pictured on pages 66 and 67.

Peanut Butter Pizzazz

Besides making wonderful sandwiches, peanut butter is a boon for cookie bakers. It gives many drop cookies, bars, brownies, cutouts and filled treats a rich, nutty flavor. For the chewy texture of nuts in your cookies, use the chunky type, or for a real splurge, the super-chunky type. Honey-roasted peanut butter works well in place of regular peanut butter.

fudgy peanut butter bars

CRUST

1½ cups all-purpose flour

¾ cup finely chopped dry roasted peanuts

½ cup packed brown sugar

½ cup (1 stick) butter or margarine, melted

TOPPING

2 cups (12-ounce package) NESTLÉ® TOLL HOUSE® Semi-Sweet Chocolate Morsels

¾ cup creamy or chunky peanut butter

⅓ cup sifted powdered sugar

For Crust:

COMBINE flour, peanuts, brown sugar and butter in ungreased 13 x 9-inch baking pan; press onto bottom of pan. Bake in preheated 350°F. oven for 10 to 12 minutes or until crust is light brown around edges.

For Topping:

MICROWAVE morsels and peanut butter in medium, microwave-safe bowl on HIGH (100%) power for 1 minute; stir. Microwave at additional 10- to 20-second intervals, stirring until smooth. Add powdered sugar; stir vigorously until smooth. Spread over hot cookie base. Chill just until chocolate is no longer shiny. Cut into bars. Serve at room temperature. Makes 3 dozen bars.

hoosier bars

1½ cups all-purpose flour

1 teaspoon baking soda

1 cup packed brown sugar, *divided*

½ cup granulated sugar

½ cup (1 stick) butter or margarine, softened

2 eggs, separated

1 teaspoon vanilla extract

2 cups (12-ounce package) NESTLÉ® TOLL HOUSE® Semi-Sweet Chocolate Morsels, *divided*

¾ cup honey-roasted peanuts, *divided*

COMBINE flour and baking soda in small bowl. Beat ½ *cup* brown sugar, granulated sugar and butter in large mixer bowl until creamy. Beat in egg yolks and vanilla extract. Gradually beat in flour mixture until crumbly. Stir in 1½ *cups* morsels and ½ *cup* peanuts. Press onto bottom of greased 13 x 9-inch baking pan.

BEAT egg whites in small mixer bowl until soft peaks form. Gradually beat in *remaining* brown sugar until stiff peaks form (see photo and tip, *page 102*); spread mixture over dough. Sprinkle with *remaining* morsels and *remaining* peanuts.

BAKE in preheated 325°F. oven for 35 to 40 minutes or until top is set and lightly browned. Cool in pan on wire rack for 20 minutes. Cut into bars while still warm. Makes 3 dozen bars.

rocky road squares

1 package (21½ ounces) fudge brownie mix calling for ½ cup water

Vegetable oil, per package directions

Egg(s), per package directions

½ cup NESTLÉ® CARNATION® Evaporated Milk

2 cups miniature marshmallows

1½ cups coarsely chopped walnuts

1 cup (6 ounces) NESTLÉ® TOLL HOUSE® Semi-Sweet Chocolate Morsels

PREPARE brownie mix according to package directions, using oil and egg(s), except substitute evaporated milk for water. Spread into greased 13 x 9-inch baking pan.

BAKE according to package directions; do not overbake. Remove from oven. Top with marshmallows, walnuts and morsels.

BAKE for 3 to 5 minutes or just until topping is warmed and beginning to melt. Cool in pan on wire rack for 20 to 30 minutes. Cut into squares. Serve warm. Makes 2 dozen squares.

Rocky Road Squares (see recipe above),
Mini Morsel Shortbread Squares (see recipe, page 74) and
Peanut Butter-Chocolate Layer Bars (see recipe, page 75)

mini morsel
shortbread squares

  1 cup (2 sticks) butter or margarine, softened
  ¾ cup granulated sugar
  1 egg
  1 teaspoon vanilla extract
  2¼ cups all-purpose flour
  2 cups (12-ounce package) NESTLÉ® TOLL HOUSE®
    Semi-Sweet Chocolate Mini Morsels, *divided*

BEAT butter and granulated sugar in large mixer bowl until creamy. Beat in egg and vanilla extract. Gradually beat in flour. Stir in *1 cup* morsels. Press into bottom of ungreased 13 x 9-inch baking pan.

BAKE in preheated 350°F. oven for 30 to 33 minutes or just until top begins to brown. Immediately sprinkle with *remaining* morsels. Let stand for 5 minutes or until morsels are shiny; spread. Cool completely in pan on wire rack. Cut shortbread into squares. Makes 4 dozen squares.

Pictured on page 73.

Creative Cuts

For a creative flair with cookies and brownies, cut them into shapes other than standard rectangles and squares. To make triangles, cut bars into 3-inch squares; cut each square in half diagonally. For diamonds, cut parallel lines 2 inches apart across the length of the pan; cut diagonal lines 2 inches apart. For extra fun, cut brownies and bars (choose less-crumbly bars) with cookie cutters.

peanut butter-chocolate layer bars

20   peanut butter sandwich cookies, finely crushed
       (about 2 cups)
 3   tablespoons butter or margarine, melted
1¼ cups lightly salted dry-roasted peanuts, chopped
 1   cup (6 ounces) NESTLÉ® TOLL HOUSE® Semi-Sweet
       Chocolate Morsels
 1   cup flaked coconut
1¼ cups (14-ounce can) NESTLÉ® CARNATION® Sweetened
       Condensed Milk

COMBINE cookie crumbs and butter in small bowl; press into
bottom of greased 13 x 9-inch baking pan. Layer peanuts, morsels
and coconut over crumb mixture. Drizzle sweetened condensed
milk evenly over top.

BAKE in preheated 350°F. oven for 20 to 25 minutes or until
coconut is golden brown. Cool completely in pan on wire rack. Cut
into bars. Makes 2 dozen bars.

Pictured on page 73.

butterscotch fudge squares

COOKIE BASE

- 1 cup all-purpose flour
- 1 cup quick or old-fashioned oats
- ¾ cup packed brown sugar
- ½ cup chopped walnuts
- ½ cup flaked coconut
- ¾ teaspoon pumpkin pie spice
- ½ teaspoon baking soda
- ¾ cup (1½ sticks) butter or margarine, melted

FUDGE

- 1½ cups granulated sugar
- ⅔ cup NESTLÉ® CARNATION® Evaporated Milk
- ½ cup LIBBY'S® Solid Pack Pumpkin
- 2 tablespoons butter or margarine
- 1½ teaspoons pumpkin pie spice
- ¼ teaspoon salt
- 2 cups (4 ounces) mini marshmallows
- 1⅔ cups (11-ounce package) NESTLÉ® TOLL HOUSE® Butterscotch Morsels
- ¾ cup chopped walnuts, *divided*
- 1 teaspoon vanilla extract

For Cookie Base:

COMBINE flour, oats, brown sugar, walnuts, coconut, pumpkin pie spice and baking soda in medium bowl. Stir in melted butter, mixing well. Press into foil-lined 15 x 10-inch jelly-roll pan. Bake in preheated 350°F. oven for 13 to 15 minutes or until slightly brown. Cool in pan on wire rack.

For Fudge:

COMBINE granulated sugar, evaporated milk, pumpkin, butter, pumpkin pie spice and salt in medium, *heavy-duty* saucepan. Bring to a boil over medium heat, stirring constantly. Boil for 8 to 10 minutes, stirring constantly. Remove from heat.

STIR IN marshmallows, morsels, *½ cup* walnuts and vanilla extract. Stir vigorously for 1 minute or until marshmallows are melted. Pour over cooled cookie base; sprinkle with *remaining* walnuts. Chill until firm. Cut into squares. Makes 4 dozen squares.

Clockwise from top right: Pumpkin Carrot Swirl Bars (see recipe, page 79), Butterscotch Fudge Squares (see recipe above) and Pumpkin Layer Bars (see recipe, page 78)

pumpkin layer bars

  ¾ cup all-purpose flour
  ⅓ cup packed brown sugar
  ⅓ cup quick or old-fashioned oats
  ¼ cup chopped nuts
1½ teaspoons ground cinnamon
  ⅓ cup butter or margarine, melted
1¼ cups LIBBY'S® Solid Pack Pumpkin
  1 cup NESTLÉ® CARNATION® Evaporated Milk
  ½ cup granulated sugar
  1 egg
  ¾ teaspoon pumpkin pie spice
  ¼ teaspoon salt
  4 ounces cream cheese, softened
  ¼ cup sour cream, at room temperature
  2 tablespoons orange marmalade

COMBINE flour, brown sugar, oats, nuts and cinnamon in medium bowl. Stir in butter, mixing well. Press onto bottom of 9-inch square baking pan. Bake in preheated 350°F. oven for 20 to 25 minutes or until golden brown. Remove from oven.

COMBINE pumpkin, evaporated milk, granulated sugar, egg, pumpkin pie spice and salt in medium bowl. Pour over oat mixture; bake at 350°F. for 20 to 25 minutes or until knife inserted near center comes out clean. Cool completely in pan on wire rack.

COMBINE cream cheese and sour cream in small bowl. Stir in orange marmalade. Spread over pumpkin layer. Chill. Cut into bars. Makes 2 dozen bars.

Pictured on page 76.

pumpkin carrot swirl bars

Lower Fat

2 cups all-purpose flour
2¼ teaspoons pumpkin pie spice
2 teaspoons baking powder
1 teaspoon baking soda
⅓ cup butter or margarine, softened
1 cup granulated sugar
½ cup packed brown sugar
1¾ cups (15-ounce can) LIBBY'S® Solid Pack Pumpkin
1 cup finely shredded carrots
2 eggs
2 egg whites
Cream Cheese Topping (recipe follows)

COMBINE flour, pumpkin pie spice, baking powder and baking soda in small bowl.

BEAT butter, granulated sugar and brown sugar in large mixer bowl until crumbly. Beat in pumpkin, carrots, eggs and egg whites until well mixed. Gradually beat in flour mixture. Spread into greased 15 x 10-inch jelly-roll pan. Dollop with teaspoonfuls of Cream Cheese Topping; swirl with spoon to marbleize.

BAKE in preheated 350°F. oven for 25 to 30 minutes or until wooden pick inserted in center comes out clean. Cool completely in pan on wire rack. Cut into bars. Makes 4 dozen bars. About 80 calories and 3 grams fat per bar.

For Cream Cheese Topping:
BEAT 4 ounces softened light cream cheese (Neufchâtel), ¼ cup granulated sugar and 1 tablespoon milk in small mixer bowl until combined.

Pictured on page 76.

white chip
meringue dessert squares

CRUST
- 2 cups all-purpose flour
- ½ cup powdered sugar
- 1 cup (2 sticks) butter or margarine, softened

TOPPING
- 2 cups (12-ounce package) NESTLÉ® TOLL HOUSE® Premier White Morsels
- 1¼ cups sliced or chopped nuts, *divided*
- 3 egg whites
- 1 cup packed brown sugar

For Crust:
COMBINE flour and powdered sugar in a medium bowl. Cut in butter with pastry blender or 2 knives until mixture resembles coarse crumbs. Press onto bottom of ungreased 13 x 9-inch baking pan. Bake crust in preheated 375°F. oven for 10 to 12 minutes or until set.

For Topping:
SPRINKLE morsels and *1 cup* nuts over hot crust. Beat egg whites in small mixer bowl until frothy. Gradually add brown sugar. Beat until stiff peaks form (see photo and tip, *page 102*). Gently spread egg white mixture over morsels and nuts. Sprinkle with *remaining* nuts.

BAKE at 375°F. for 15 to 20 minutes or until golden brown. Serve warm or cool. Cut into bars. Makes 2 dozen squares.

sour cream walnut bars

2 cups all-purpose flour
2 teaspoons ground cinnamon
1 teaspoon baking powder
1 teaspoon baking soda
1 teaspoon ground ginger
¾ teaspoon salt
½ teaspoon ground allspice
1½ cups granulated sugar
1 cup sour cream
½ cup (1 stick) butter or margarine, softened
2 eggs
1 cup LIBBY'S® Solid Pack Pumpkin
2 teaspoons vanilla extract
½ cup chopped nuts
Butter Icing (recipe follows)

COMBINE flour, cinnamon, baking powder, baking soda, ginger, salt and allspice in medium bowl. Beat sugar, sour cream, butter and eggs in large mixer bowl until blended. Beat in pumpkin and vanilla extract. Gradually beat in flour mixture. Stir in nuts. Spread batter into greased and floured 15 x 10-inch jelly-roll pan.

BAKE in preheated 375°F. oven for 20 to 25 minutes or until wooden pick inserted in center comes out clean. Cool completely in pan on wire rack; spread with Butter Icing. Cut into bars. Makes 4 dozen bars.

For Butter Icing:
HEAT ⅓ cup butter in medium saucepan over medium heat, stirring until melted; remove from heat. Stir in 3 cups sifted powdered sugar and 1 teaspoon vanilla extract. Stir in 4 to 6 tablespoons milk until icing is of spreading consistency.

chocolate cinnamon nut bars

COOKIE CRUST

    2 cups all-purpose flour
    ¾ cup (1½ sticks) butter or margarine, softened
    ⅓ cup granulated sugar
    ¾ teaspoon baking powder
    ¾ teaspoon ground cinnamon
  1½ cups chopped nuts

CHOCOLATE LAYER

    1 cup (6 ounces) NESTLÉ® TOLL HOUSE® Semi-Sweet
       Chocolate Morsels
    ¼ cup (½ stick) butter or margarine, cut into pieces
  1¼ cups packed light brown sugar
    3 eggs
    1 teaspoon vanilla extract
       Sifted powdered sugar

For Cookie Crust:
BEAT flour, butter, granulated sugar, baking powder and cinnamon
in large mixer bowl until mixture is crumbly. Stir in nuts. Press
onto bottom of ungreased 13 x 9-inch baking pan. Bake in
preheated 350°F. oven for 15 to 18 minutes or until firm.

For Chocolate Layer:
MELT morsels and butter in medium, *heavy-duty* saucepan over
lowest possible heat, stirring constantly until smooth. Remove
from heat; stir in brown sugar, eggs and vanilla extract. Pour
over hot crust.

BAKE at 350°F. for 20 to 25 minutes or until center is set. Cool
completely in pan on wire rack. Sprinkle with powdered sugar. Cut
into bars. Makes 2½ dozen bars.

*Top to bottom: White Chip Brownies (see recipe, page 64),
Chocolate Cinnamon Nut Bars (see recipe above) and
Chocolate Walnut Pie Bars (see recipe, page 84)*

chocolate walnut pie bars

CRUST
1½ cups all-purpose flour
 ½ cup (1 stick) butter or margarine, softened
 ¼ cup packed brown sugar
FILLING
  3 eggs
 ¾ cup light corn syrup
 ¾ cup granulated sugar
  2 tablespoons butter or margarine, melted
  1 teaspoon vanilla extract
  2 cups (12-ounce package) NESTLÉ® TOLL HOUSE®
      Semi-Sweet Chocolate Morsels
1½ cups coarsely chopped walnuts

For Crust:
BEAT flour, butter and brown sugar in small mixer bowl until crumbly. Press onto bottom of greased 13 x 9-inch baking pan. Bake in preheated 350°F. oven for 12 to 15 minutes or until lightly browned.

For Filling:
BEAT together eggs, corn syrup, granulated sugar, butter and vanilla extract in large mixer bowl. Stir in morsels and walnuts; pour over hot crust.

BAKE at 350°F. for 25 to 30 minutes or until center is set. Cool completely in pan on wire rack. Cut into bars. Makes 3 dozen bars.

Pictured on page 82.

banana bars

2 cups all-purpose flour
2 teaspoons baking powder
½ teaspoon salt
¾ cup (1½ sticks) butter or margarine, softened
⅔ cup granulated sugar
⅔ cup packed brown sugar
1 teaspoon vanilla extract
1 cup (2 bananas) mashed ripe banana
1 egg
2 cups (12-ounce package) NESTLÉ® TOLL HOUSE® Semi-Sweet Chocolate Mini Morsels
Sifted powdered sugar

COMBINE flour, baking powder and salt in medium bowl. Beat butter, granulated sugar, brown sugar and vanilla extract in large mixer bowl until creamy. Beat in bananas and egg. Gradually beat in flour mixture. Stir in morsels. Spread into greased 15 x 10-inch jelly-roll pan.

BAKE in preheated 350°F. oven for 20 to 30 minutes or until wooden pick inserted in center comes out clean. Cool completely in pan on wire rack. Sprinkle with powdered sugar. Cut into bars. Makes 6 dozen bars.

chocolate chip cookie brittle

1 cup (2 sticks) butter or margarine, softened
1 cup granulated sugar
1½ teaspoons vanilla extract
1 teaspoon salt
2 cups all-purpose flour
2 cups (12-ounce package) NESTLÉ® TOLL HOUSE®
   Semi-Sweet Chocolate Morsels, *divided*
1 cup chopped nuts*

BEAT butter, granulated sugar, vanilla extract and salt in large mixer bowl. Gradually beat in flour. Stir in *1½ cups* morsels and nuts. Press into ungreased 15 x 10-inch jelly-roll pan.

BAKE in preheated 375°F. oven for 20 to 25 minutes or until golden brown and set. Cool in pan until just slightly warm.

MICROWAVE *remaining* morsels in heavy-duty plastic bag on HIGH (100%) power for 1 minute; knead bag to mix. Microwave at additional 10-second intervals, kneading until smooth. Cut a small hole in corner of bag; squeeze to drizzle over cookie brittle. Allow chocolate to cool and set; break into irregular pieces. Makes about 2¼ pounds.

*Note: Omitting nuts could cause the brittle to become dry.

Clockwise from top right:
Super Easy Chocolate Triangles (see recipe, page 88),
Easy Butterscotch Chip Cookies (see recipe, page 25),
Chewy Cocoa Brownies (see recipe, page 59) and
Chocolate Chip Cookie Brittle (see recipe above)

super easy chocolate triangles

20 chocolate sandwich cookies, finely crushed (about 2 cups)

1½ cups chopped nuts

1½ cups (9 ounces) NESTLÉ® TOLL HOUSE® Semi-Sweet Chocolate Morsels

1 cup flaked coconut

1¼ cups (14-ounce can) NESTLÉ® CARNATION® Sweetened Condensed Milk

PRESS crushed cookies onto bottom of greased 13 x 9-inch baking pan; sprinkle with nuts, morsels and coconut. Drizzle with sweetened condensed milk.

BAKE in preheated 350°F. oven for 20 to 25 minutes or until coconut is golden brown around edges. Cool completely in pan on wire rack. Cut into squares; cut each square in half diagonally to form a triangle. Makes 3½ dozen triangles.

Pictured on page 86.

Crush Cookies the Easy Way

To crush cookies quickly and easily, place them in a large, heavy-duty plastic bag. Seal the bag. Crush the cookies by rolling over them with a rolling pin until the pieces are the size of fine crumbs. The crumbs stay neatly in the bag and don't mess up your kitchen counter or floor.

lemon bars

CRUST

- 2 cups all-purpose flour
- ½ cup powdered sugar
- 1 cup (2 sticks) butter or margarine, softened

FILLING

- 4 eggs
- 1¼ cups (14-ounce can) NESTLÉ® CARNATION® Sweetened Condensed Milk
- ⅔ cup lemon juice
- 1 tablespoon all-purpose flour
- 1 teaspoon baking powder
- ¼ teaspoon salt
- 4 drops yellow food coloring (optional)
- 1 tablespoon grated lemon peel
- Sifted powdered sugar (optional)

For Crust:

COMBINE flour and sugar in medium bowl. Cut in butter with pastry blender or two knives until mixture is crumbly. Press lightly onto bottom and halfway up sides of ungreased 13 x 9-inch baking pan. Bake in preheated 350°F. oven for 20 minutes.

For Filling:

BEAT eggs and sweetened condensed milk in large mixer bowl until fluffy. Beat in lemon juice, flour, baking powder, salt and food coloring just until blended. Fold in lemon peel; pour over crust.

BAKE at 350°F. for 20 to 25 minutes or until set and crust is brown. Cool in pan on wire rack; chill for about 2 hours. Sprinkle with powdered sugar. Cut into bars or, for round shapes, use biscuit or cookie cutter. Makes 4 dozen bars.

chocolate butterscotch cereal bars

1 cup granulated sugar
1 cup light corn syrup
1 cup creamy peanut butter
6 cups crisp rice cereal
1 cup (6 ounces) NESTLÉ® TOLL HOUSE® Semi-Sweet Chocolate Morsels
1 cup (6 ounces) NESTLÉ® TOLL HOUSE® Butterscotch Morsels

COMBINE granulated sugar and corn syrup in large saucepan; bring *just to a boil* over medium heat, stirring constantly. Remove from heat; stir in peanut butter. Stir in cereal. Press into greased 13 x 9-inch baking pan.

MICROWAVE chocolate and butterscotch morsels in medium, microwave-safe bowl on HIGH (100%) power for 1 minute; stir. Microwave at additional 10- to 20-second intervals, stirring until smooth. Spread over cereal mixture. Chill in pan for 20 minutes or until firm. Cut into bars. Makes 4 dozen bars.

Coffee Bar

End a wonderful evening with cookies and coffee by the fire or another cozy spot. This is easy to do with a well-dressed coffee bar, where guests can embellish their cups with a variety of finishing touches.

Coffee: CAFÉ SARKS Ground Coffees, such as French Roast, Mocha Java and Vanilla Nut Creme.

Sugar and Spice: NESTLÉ® CARNATION® COFFEE-MATE® Non-Dairy Flavored Creamers, sugar cubes, NESTLÉ® TOLL HOUSE® Semi-Sweet Chocolate Baking Bar shavings, cinnamon sticks or ground nutmeg.

Flavored Liqueurs: Coffee, orange, hazelnut or almond.

Bar Cookie Bonanza

When you're in the mood for cookies, there's nothing easier than bar cookies—just mix, bake and cut into pieces. For surefire success with your bar cookies, follow these baking rules of the road:

Using the right size baking pan is critical when making bar cookies. A pan that is too large or too small will alter the baking time and texture of the bars. So, use the size pan called for in the recipe. If you don't have the size pan recommended, here are some substitutions to try. In place of a 15 x 10-inch jelly-roll pan, use two 9 x 9-inch baking pans. For a 13 x 9-inch baking pan, substitute two 8 x 8-inch baking pans. Use the oven temperature specified in the recipe and check for doneness about 5 minutes before the specified minimum baking time.

Make cleanup and storage a breeze. Line the baking pan with foil, extending the foil over the edges of the pan. If the recipe calls for a greased pan, grease the foil instead. Spread the cookie dough evenly in the foil liner. Bake the bars and cool them in the pan. To remove the bars, pull the foil edges down to the counter and lift the bars out. If you want to freeze or store the bars, simply wrap them in the foil. To serve the bars, cut them as directed in the recipe.

Cut evenly shaped bars by using a ruler to measure and wooden picks to mark the lines for cutting into the bars. Using a long knife, cut straight down along the lines, wiping the knife between cuts. Separate the bars by removing one of the corners first.

Dress up unfrosted bars with a dusting of powdered sugar (see Sift on a Sugar Stencil, page 59), a sprinkle of ground spice or a drizzle of chocolate (see Dazzle with a Drizzle, page 234). For frosted bars, add a decorative touch by sprinkling on NESTLÉ® TOLL HOUSE® Semi-Sweet Chocolate Mini-Morsels, chopped nuts, toasted coconut or chopped, dried or candied fruit pieces.

iced pumpkin blondies

2¼ cups all-purpose flour
2½ teaspoons baking powder
 2 teaspoons ground cinnamon
¼ teaspoon salt
¾ cup (1½ sticks) butter or margarine, softened
1½ cups packed brown sugar
 1 teaspoon vanilla extract
 2 eggs
 1 cup LIBBY'S® Solid Pack Pumpkin
   Maple Icing (recipe follows)

COMBINE flour, baking powder, cinnamon and salt in medium bowl. Beat butter, brown sugar and vanilla extract in large mixer bowl until creamy. Add eggs, one at a time, beating well after each addition. Beat in pumpkin. Gradually beat in flour mixture. Spread into greased 15 x 10-inch jelly-roll pan.

BAKE in preheated 350°F. oven for 20 to 25 minutes or until wooden pick inserted in center comes out clean. Cool completely in pan on wire rack; spread with Maple Icing. Cut into bars. Makes 4 dozen bars.

For Maple Icing:
BEAT 2 packages (3 ounces *each*) softened cream cheese and 2 tablespoons softened butter or margarine in small mixer bowl; gradually beat in 2 cups sifted powdered sugar. Beat in 1 to 2 teaspoons maple flavoring until fluffy.

lower-fat blonde brownies

2¼ cups all-purpose flour
2½ teaspoons baking powder
½ teaspoon salt
1¾ cups packed brown sugar
6 tablespoons (¾ stick) margarine, softened
3 egg whites
1½ teaspoons vanilla extract
⅓ cup water
2 cups (12-ounce package) NESTLÉ® TOLL HOUSE®
Semi-Sweet Chocolate Morsels

COMBINE flour, baking powder and salt in small bowl. Beat brown sugar, margarine, egg whites and vanilla extract in large mixer bowl until smooth. Gradually beat in flour mixture alternately with water. Stir in morsels. Spread into greased 15 x 10-inch jelly-roll pan.

BAKE in preheated 350°F. oven for 20 to 25 minutes or until top is golden brown. Cool completely in pan on wire rack. Cut into squares; cut each in half diagonally to form triangles. Makes 3 dozen brownies. About 140 calories and 5 grams fat per brownie.

blonde brownies

2¼ cups all-purpose flour
2½ teaspoons baking powder
½ teaspoon salt
1¾ cups packed brown sugar
¾ cup (1½ sticks) butter or margarine, softened
1 teaspoon vanilla extract
3 eggs
2 cups (12-ounce package) NESTLÉ® TOLL HOUSE®
Semi-Sweet Chocolate Morsels

COMBINE flour, baking powder and salt in small bowl. Beat brown sugar, butter and vanilla extract in large mixer bowl until creamy. Add eggs, one at a time, beating well after each addition. Gradually beat in flour mixture. Stir in morsels. Spread into greased 15 x 10-inch jelly-roll pan.

BAKE in preheated 350°F. oven for 20 to 25 minutes or until top is golden brown. Cool completely in pan on wire rack. Cut into bars. Makes 35 brownies.

fruit and chocolate dream bars

CRUST

1¼ cups all-purpose flour

½ cup granulated sugar

½ cup (1 stick) butter or margarine

TOPPING

⅔ cup all-purpose flour

½ cup chopped pecans

⅓ cup packed brown sugar

6 tablespoons (¾ stick) butter or margarine, softened

½ cup raspberry or strawberry jam

2 cups (11½-ounce package) NESTLÉ® TOLL HOUSE® Milk Chocolate Morsels

For Crust:
COMBINE flour and granulated sugar in medium bowl. Cut in butter with pastry blender or 2 knives until mixture resembles coarse crumbs. Press onto bottom of greased 9-inch square baking pan. Bake in preheated 375°F. oven for 18 to 22 minutes or until set but not brown.

For Topping:
COMBINE flour, pecans and brown sugar in same bowl. Cut in butter with pastry blender or 2 knives until mixture resembles coarse crumbs.

SPREAD jam over hot crust. Sprinkle with topping and morsels. Bake at 375°F. for 15 to 20 minutes or until golden brown. Cool completely in pan on wire rack. Cut into bars. Makes 2½ dozen.

holiday cookies

like gift giving and family gatherings, baking and sharing cookies is a holiday tradition, with treasured recipes passed from friend to friend and handed down through generations. Add to your collection of special-occasion cookies with the festive treats in this chapter.

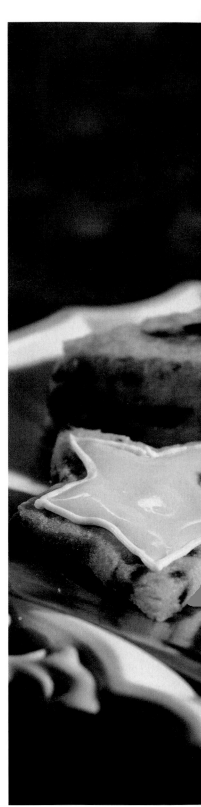

Chocolate Cherry Thumbprints (see recipe, page 114), Chocolate Raspberry Layer Bars (see recipe, page 100), Chocolate Mini Chip Holiday Cookies (see recipe, page 101) and Swirl-of-Chocolate Cheesecake Triangles (see recipe, page 115)

chocolate raspberry layer bars

1⅔ cups graham cracker crumbs

½ cup (1 stick) butter or margarine, melted

2 cups (12-ounce package) NESTLÉ® TOLL HOUSE® Semi-Sweet Chocolate Morsels, *divided*

2⅔ cups (7-ounce package) flaked coconut

1¼ cups (14-ounce can) NESTLÉ® CARNATION® Sweetened Condensed Milk

1 cup seedless red raspberry jam

⅓ cup finely chopped walnuts (optional)

⅓ cup NESTLÉ® TOLL HOUSE® Premier White Morsels

COMBINE graham cracker crumbs and butter in medium bowl. Press firmly onto bottom of ungreased 13 x 9-inch baking pan. Sprinkle with *1½ cups* semi-sweet morsels, then coconut; pour sweetened condensed milk evenly over top.

BAKE in preheated 350°F. oven for 20 to 25 minutes or until lightly browned; cool completely in pan on wire rack.

SPREAD jam over cooled top; sprinkle with walnuts. Place *remaining* semi-sweet morsels and white morsels in separate heavy-duty plastic bags. Microwave together on MEDIUM-HIGH (70%) power for 45 seconds; knead bags to mix. Microwave at additional 10-second intervals, kneading until smooth. Cut a small hole in corner of each bag; squeeze to pipe over bars. Chill for 5 minutes to set chocolate. Cut into bars. Makes 2 dozen bars.

Pictured on pages 98 and 99.

chocolate mini chip holiday cookies

　1　cup (2 sticks) butter or margarine, softened
　½　cup packed brown sugar
　⅓　cup granulated sugar
　2　teaspoons vanilla extract
　½　teaspoon salt
　1　egg yolk
2½　cups all-purpose flour
　2　cups (12-ounce package) NESTLÉ® TOLL HOUSE® Semi-Sweet Chocolate Mini-Morsels, *divided*
　1　container (16 ounces) prepared vanilla frosting, colored if desired
　　Chocolate Drizzle (optional recipe follows)

BEAT butter, brown sugar, granulated sugar, vanilla extract and salt in large mixer bowl until creamy. Beat in egg yolk. Gradually beat in flour. Stir in *1½ cups* morsels. Divide dough in half. Cover; chill for 1 hour or until firm.

ROLL ½ of dough to ¼-inch thickness between 2 sheets of waxed paper. Remove top sheet of waxed paper. Cut dough into shapes (see Cookie Creativity, *page 131*). Lift from waxed paper; place on ungreased baking sheets. Chill for 10 minutes. Repeat with remaining dough.

BAKE in preheated 350°F. oven for 9 to 11 minutes or until golden brown. Let stand for 2 minutes; remove to wire racks to cool completely. Spread or pipe with frosting as desired (see Cookie Decorating Tips, *page 56*). Decorate with Chocolate Drizzle, if desired. Makes about 3 dozen cookies.

For Chocolate Drizzle:
PLACE *remaining* morsels in heavy-duty plastic bag. Microwave on HIGH (100%) power for 45 seconds; knead bag to mix. Microwave at additional 10-second intervals, kneading until smooth. Cut a small hole in corner of bag; squeeze to pipe chocolate over frosted cookies.

Pictured on pages 98 and 99.

mini morsel meringue cookies

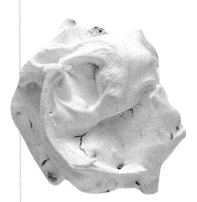

4 egg whites
½ teaspoon salt
½ teaspoon cream of tartar
1 cup granulated sugar
2 cups (12-ounce package) NESTLÉ® TOLL HOUSE®
　Semi-Sweet Chocolate Mini-Morsels

BEAT egg whites, salt and cream of tartar in small mixer bowl until soft peaks form. Gradually beat in granulated sugar until stiff peaks form (see photo, *below*). Gently fold in morsels, ⅓ at a time. Drop by level tablespoon onto greased baking sheets.

BAKE in preheated 300°F. oven for 20 to 25 minutes or until cookies are dry and crisp.

LET STAND for 2 minutes; remove to wire racks to cool completely. Store in airtight containers. Makes about 5 dozen cookies.

For stiff peaks, continue beating the egg-white mixture, gradually adding the sugar, until the mixture looks glossy and the peaks stand straight when the beaters are lifted.

mini chip snowball cookies

1½ cups (3 sticks) butter or margarine, softened
¾ cup powdered sugar
1 tablespoon vanilla extract
½ teaspoon salt
3 cups all-purpose flour
2 cups (12-ounce package) NESTLÉ® TOLL HOUSE®
    Semi-Sweet Chocolate Mini-Morsels
½ cup finely chopped nuts
    Powdered sugar

BEAT butter, ¾ cup powdered sugar, vanilla extract and salt in large mixer bowl until creamy. Gradually beat in flour. Stir in morsels and nuts. Shape level tablespoonfuls of dough into 1-inch balls. Place on ungreased baking sheets.

BAKE in preheated 375°F. oven for 10 to 12 minutes or until cookies are set and lightly browned. Remove from oven. Sift sugar over hot cookies on baking sheet. Let stand for 10 minutes; remove to wire racks to cool completely. Sprinkle with additional sugar, if desired. Store cookies in airtight containers. Makes about 5 dozen cookies.

cream cheese-chocolate chip pastry cookies

1 package (17¼ ounces) frozen puff pastry, thawed
1 package (8 ounces) cream cheese, softened
3 tablespoons granulated sugar
2 cups (11½-ounce package) NESTLÉ® TOLL HOUSE® Milk
  Chocolate Morsels, *divided*

ROLL 1 sheet puff pastry to 14 x 10-inch rectangle on floured surface. Combine cream cheese and granulated sugar in small bowl.

SPREAD half of cream cheese mixture over puff pastry, leaving 1-inch border on 1 long side. Sprinkle with *1 cup* morsels. Roll up, starting at long side covered with cream cheese. Seal edge by dampening with water. Repeat with *remaining* ingredients. Chill for 1 hour. Cut rolls crosswise into 1-inch-thick slices. Place cut side up on parchment-paper-lined or lightly greased baking sheets.

BAKE in preheated 375°F. oven for 20 to 25 minutes or until golden brown. Let stand for 2 minutes; remove to wire racks to cool completely. Makes about 2 dozen cookies.

Puff Pastry Pointers

Ultra flaky puff pastry is the secret ingredient for many buttery, rich desserts and cookies such as Cream Cheese-Chocolate Chip Pastry Cookies (see above). For best results, thaw the pastry at room temperature according to package directions. Cover and refrigerate one of the sheets while working with the other. After assembling the cookie rolls, chill them for 1 hour so they are firm enough to slice easily. To avoid crushing the puff pastry rolls as you cut the slices, use a sharp knife, such as a chef's knife, to cut straight down through the rolls. Don't pull the knife or cut the rolls at a slant because this causes the edges of the pastry to puff unevenly during baking.

chocolate chip mexican wedding cakes

- 1 cup (2 sticks) butter, softened
- ½ cup sifted powdered sugar
- 1 teaspoon vanilla extract
- 2 cups all-purpose flour
- ⅔ cup finely chopped nuts
- 2 to 2½ teaspoons ground cinnamon
- 2 cups (12-ounce package) NESTLÉ® TOLL HOUSE® Semi-Sweet Chocolate Morsels, *divided*

BEAT butter and powdered sugar in large mixer bowl until creamy. Beat in vanilla extract. Gradually beat in flour, nuts and cinnamon. Stir in *1½ cups* morsels. Roll dough into 1-inch balls; place on ungreased baking sheets.

BAKE in preheated 350°F. oven for 10 to 12 minutes or until set and light golden brown on bottom. Let stand for 2 minutes; remove to wire racks to cool completely.

PLACE *remaining* morsels in heavy-duty plastic bag. Microwave on HIGH (100%) power for 30 seconds; knead bag to mix. Microwave at additional 10- to 20-second intervals, kneading until smooth. Cut a small hole in corner of bag; squeeze to drizzle chocolate over cookies. Chill cookies for 5 minutes or until chocolate is set. Store in airtight containers at room temperature. Makes about 4½ dozen cookies.

star of david chocolate cookies

2 cups all-purpose flour
½ cup NESTLÉ® TOLL HOUSE® Baking Cocoa
¼ teaspoon salt
1 cup (2 sticks) butter or margarine, softened
1 cup powdered sugar
1 teaspoon vanilla extract
1 container (16 ounces) prepared vanilla frosting

COMBINE flour, cocoa and salt in small bowl. Beat butter, powdered sugar and vanilla extract in large mixer bowl until creamy. Gradually beat in cocoa mixture. Shape dough into 2 balls. Roll each ball of dough between two sheets waxed paper to ¼-inch thickness. Cut with 2-inch star-shaped cookie cutter. Place on ungreased baking sheets; pierce with fork.

BAKE in preheated 350°F. oven for 8 to 10 minutes or until set. Let stand for 2 minutes; remove to wire racks to cool completely. Decorate with frosting (see Cookie Decorating Tips, *page 56*). Makes about 3 dozen cookies.

Special Delivery

An old-fashioned tin, decorative basket, colorful canister or eye-catching gift bag brimming with homemade cookies makes a thoughtful gift. If the container you've chosen doesn't have a tight-fitting lid, keep the cookies fresh by wrapping them in plastic wrap or placing them in a zip-top plastic bag before adding them to the container. Add color to your package by lining the container with festive tissue paper or napkins. For open containers, such as baskets, overwrap the entire container with colored cellophane or plastic wrap tied with a ribbon.

chocolate almond biscotti

2 cups (12-ounce package) NESTLÉ® TOLL HOUSE® Semi-Sweet Chocolate Morsels, *divided*

2 cups all-purpose flour

1/4 cup NESTLÉ® TOLL HOUSE® Baking Cocoa

1 1/2 teaspoons baking powder

1/4 teaspoon baking soda

1/4 teaspoon salt

1/2 cup granulated sugar

1/2 cup packed brown sugar

1/4 cup (1/2 stick) butter or margarine, softened

1/2 teaspoon vanilla extract

1/2 teaspoon almond extract

3 eggs

1 cup slivered almonds, toasted

Chocolate Coating (optional recipe follows)

MICROWAVE *1 cup* morsels in small, microwave-safe bowl on HIGH (100%) power 1 minute; stir. Microwave at additional 10- to 20-second intervals, stirring until smooth. Cool to room temperature.

COMBINE flour, cocoa, baking powder, baking soda and salt in medium bowl. Beat granulated sugar, brown sugar, butter, vanilla extract and almond extract in mixer bowl until crumbly. Add eggs, one at a time, beating well after each. Beat in melted chocolate. Gradually beat in flour mixture. Stir in almonds. Chill for 15 minutes or until firm. Shape dough with floured hands into 2 loaves (3 inches wide by 1 inch high) on 1 large or 2 small greased baking sheet(s).

BAKE in preheated 325°F. oven for 40 to 50 minutes or until firm. Let stand 15 minutes. Cut into 3/4-inch-thick slices; turn slices on their sides. Bake for 10 minutes on *each* side or until dry. Remove to wire racks to cool completely. If desired, dip each biscotti halfway into Chocolate Coating, pushing mixture up onto cookie with a spatula; shake off excess. Place on waxed-paper-lined baking sheets. Chill for 10 minutes or until chocolate is set. Store in airtight containers in cool place or chill. Makes 2 1/2 dozen biscotti.

For Chocolate Coating:
MICROWAVE *remaining* morsels and 2 tablespoons shortening in microwave-safe bowl on HIGH (100%) power for 1 minute; stir. Microwave at additional 10- to 20-second intervals, stirring until smooth.

Chocolate Almond Biscotti (see recipe above) and Chocolate-Dipped Brandy Snaps (see recipe, page 110)

chocolate-dipped brandy snaps

½ cup (1 stick) butter
½ cup granulated sugar
⅓ cup dark corn syrup
½ teaspoon ground cinnamon
¼ teaspoon ground ginger
1 cup all-purpose flour
2 teaspoons brandy
1 cup (6 ounces) NESTLÉ® TOLL HOUSE®
Semi-Sweet Chocolate Morsels
1 tablespoon shortening
⅓ cup chopped nuts

MELT butter, granulated sugar, corn syrup, cinnamon and ginger in medium saucepan over low heat, stirring until smooth. Remove from heat; stir in flour and brandy. Drop by rounded teaspoon about 3 inches apart onto ungreased baking sheets, baking no more than 6 at a time.

BAKE in preheated 300°F. oven for 10 to 14 minutes or until deep caramel color. Let stand for a few seconds. Remove from baking sheets and immediately roll around wooden spoon handle; cool.

MICROWAVE morsels and shortening in small, microwave-safe bowl on HIGH (100%) power for 45 seconds; stir. Microwave at additional 10- to 20-second intervals, stirring until smooth.

DIP each cookie halfway into melted chocolate mixture, pushing mixture up onto cookie with a spatula; shake off excess. Sprinkle with nuts; place on waxed-paper-lined baking sheets. Chill for 10 minutes or until chocolate is set. Store in airtight containers in refrigerator. Makes about 3 dozen cookies.

Pictured on page 108.

pumpkin spiced and iced cookies

2¼ cups all-purpose flour
1½ teaspoons pumpkin pie spice
1 teaspoon baking powder
½ teaspoon baking soda
½ teaspoon salt
1 cup (2 sticks) butter or margarine, softened
1 cup granulated sugar
1¾ cups (15-ounce can) LIBBY'S® Solid Pack Pumpkin
2 eggs
1 teaspoon vanilla extract
2 cups (12-ounce package) NESTLÉ® TOLL HOUSE® Semi-Sweet Chocolate Morsels
1 cup chopped walnuts (optional)
Vanilla Glaze (recipe follows)

COMBINE flour, pumpkin pie spice, baking powder, baking soda and salt in medium bowl. Beat butter and granulated sugar in large mixer bowl until creamy. Beat in pumpkin, eggs and vanilla extract. Gradually beat in flour mixture. Stir in morsels and walnuts. Drop by rounded tablespoon onto greased baking sheets.

BAKE in preheated 375°F. oven for 15 to 20 minutes or until edges are lightly browned. Let stand for 5 minutes; remove to wire racks to cool completely. Drizzle or spread with Vanilla Glaze. Makes about 5½ dozen cookies.

For Vanilla Glaze:
COMBINE 1 cup powdered sugar, 1 to 1½ tablespoons milk and ½ teaspoon vanilla extract in small bowl; mix well.

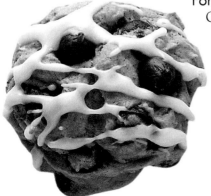

milk chocolate florentine cookies

⅔ cup butter
2 cups quick oats
1 cup granulated sugar
⅔ cup all-purpose flour
¼ cup light or dark corn syrup
¼ cup milk
1 teaspoon vanilla extract
¼ teaspoon salt
2 cups (11½-ounce package) NESTLÉ® TOLL HOUSE® Milk Chocolate Morsels

MELT butter in medium saucepan; remove from heat. Stir in oats, granulated sugar, flour, corn syrup, milk, vanilla extract and salt; mix well. Drop by level teaspoon about 3 inches apart onto foil-lined baking sheets. Spread thinly with rubber spatula.

BAKE in preheated 375°F. oven for 6 to 8 minutes or until golden brown. Cool completely on baking sheets on wire racks. Peel foil from cookies.

MICROWAVE morsels in medium, microwave-safe bowl on MEDIUM-HIGH (70%) power for 1 minute; stir. Microwave at additional 10- to 20-second intervals, stirring until smooth.

SPREAD thin layer of melted chocolate onto flat side of *half* the cookies. Top with *remaining* cookies, placing flat side against chocolate. Makes about 3½ dozen sandwich cookies.

chocolate cherry thumbprints

2 cups (12-ounce package) NESTLÉ® TOLL HOUSE® Semi-Sweet Chocolate Morsels, *divided*

1¾ cups quick or old-fashioned oats

1½ cups all-purpose flour

¼ cup NESTLÉ® TOLL HOUSE® Baking Cocoa

1 teaspoon baking powder

¼ teaspoon salt (optional)

¾ cup granulated sugar

⅔ cup butter or margarine, softened

2 eggs

1 teaspoon vanilla extract

2 cups (two 10-ounce jars) maraschino cherries, drained and patted dry

MICROWAVE *1 cup* morsels in small, microwave-safe bowl on HIGH (100%) power for 1 minute; stir. Microwave at additional 10- to 20-second intervals, stirring until smooth. Cool to room temperature. Combine oats, flour, cocoa, baking powder and salt in medium bowl. Beat granulated sugar, butter, eggs and vanilla extract in large mixer bowl until smooth. Beat in melted chocolate. Stir in oat mixture. Cover; chill dough for 1 hour. Shape dough into 1-inch balls. Place 2 inches apart on ungreased baking sheet. Press deep centers with thumb. Place maraschino cherry into each center.

BAKE in preheated 350°F. oven 10 to 12 minutes or until set. Let stand 2 minutes; remove to wire racks to cool completely. Melt *remaining* morsels as above; drizzle over cookies. Makes 4 dozen.

Pictured on pages 98 and 99.

swirl-of-chocolate cheesecake triangles

CRUST
- 2 cups graham cracker crumbs
- ½ cup (1 stick) butter or margarine, melted
- ⅓ cup granulated sugar

FILLING
- 2 packages (8 ounces *each*) cream cheese, softened
- 1 cup granulated sugar
- ¼ cup all-purpose flour

- 1½ cups (12-fluid-ounce can) NESTLÉ® CARNATION® Evaporated Milk
- 2 eggs
- 1 tablespoon vanilla extract
- 1 cup (6 ounces) NESTLÉ® TOLL HOUSE® Semi-Sweet Chocolate Morsels

For Crust:
COMBINE crumbs, butter and granulated sugar in medium bowl; press onto bottom of ungreased 13 x 9-inch baking pan.

For Filling:
BEAT cream cheese, granulated sugar and flour in large mixer bowl until smooth. Gradually beat in evaporated milk, eggs and vanilla extract.

MICROWAVE morsels in medium, microwave-safe bowl on HIGH (100%) power for 1 minute; stir. Microwave at additional 10- to 20-second intervals, stirring until smooth.

STIR *1 cup* cream cheese mixture into chocolate. Pour *remaining* cream cheese mixture over crust. Pour chocolate mixture over cream cheese mixture. Swirl mixtures with spoon, pulling plain cream cheese mixture up to surface.

BAKE in preheated 325°F. oven for 40 to 45 minutes or until set. Cool in pan to room temperature on wire rack; chill until firm. Cut into squares; cut each square in half diagonally to form triangles. Makes 2½ dozen triangles.

Pictured on pages 98 and 99.

pumpkin white chip macadamia bars

2 cups all-purpose flour
2 teaspoons ground cinnamon
1 teaspoon ground cloves
1 teaspoon baking soda
1 cup (2 sticks) butter or margarine, softened
½ cup granulated sugar
½ cup packed brown sugar
1 cup LIBBY'S® Solid Pack Pumpkin
1 egg
2 teaspoons vanilla extract
2 cups (12-ounce package) NESTLÉ® TOLL HOUSE® Premier White Morsels, *divided*
⅔ cup coarsely chopped macadamia nuts

COMBINE flour, cinnamon, cloves and baking soda in small bowl. Beat butter, granulated sugar and brown sugar in large mixer bowl until creamy. Beat in pumpkin, egg and vanilla extract until blended; gradually beat in flour mixture. Stir in 1½ *cups* morsels and nuts. Spread into greased 15 x 10-inch jelly-roll pan.

BAKE in preheated 350°F. oven for 18 to 22 minutes or until wooden pick inserted in center comes out clean. Cool in pan on wire rack.

PLACE *remaining* morsels in heavy-duty plastic bag. Microwave on MEDIUM-HIGH (70%) power for 45 seconds; knead bag to mix. Microwave at additional 10-second intervals, kneading until smooth. Cut a small hole in corner of bag; squeeze to drizzle chocolate over bars. Makes 4 dozen bars.

From bottom corner: Original Nestlé® Toll House® Chocolate Chip Cookies (see recipe, page 8), Chocolate Crinkle-Top Cookies (see recipe, page 118), Pumpkin White Chip Macadamia Bars (see recipe above) and Extra-Easy Cut-Out Cookies (see tip, page 127)

chocolate crinkle-top cookies

2 cups (12-ounce package) NESTLÉ® TOLL HOUSE®
Semi-Sweet Chocolate Morsels, *divided*

1½ cups all-purpose flour

1½ teaspoons baking powder

¼ teaspoon salt

1 cup granulated sugar

6 tablespoons butter or margarine, softened

1½ teaspoons vanilla extract

2 eggs

½ cup powdered sugar

MICROWAVE *1 cup* morsels in medium, microwave-safe bowl on
HIGH (100%) power for 1 minute; stir. Microwave at additional
10- to 20-second intervals, stirring until smooth; cool to room
temperature. Combine flour, baking powder and salt in small bowl.

BEAT granulated sugar, butter and vanilla extract in large mixer
bowl until crumbly. Beat in melted chocolate. Add eggs, one at a
time, beating well after each addition. Gradually beat in flour
mixture. Stir in *remaining* morsels. Cover; chill just until firm.
Shape dough into 1½-inch balls; roll in powdered sugar. Place on
ungreased baking sheets.

BAKE in preheated 350°F. oven for 10 to 15 minutes or until
sides are set but centers are still slightly soft. Let stand for
2 minutes; remove to wire racks to cool completely. Makes
about 3 dozen cookies.

Pictured on page 116.

Host a Holiday Cookie Exchange

When your holiday-season calendar is full, it's often difficult to find the time to bake and gather with friends. Host a cookie exchange and accomplish both. Here's how:

Decide how many people you can host comfortably. You'll need enough space to display all the cookies. If you want only a few kinds of cookies, four to six people will be plenty, but if you want a large assortment of cookies, ask 10 to 12 people to join in the exchange.

Schedule the exchange for late November or early December so your guests will have time to bake before the holiday rush.

Ask each friend to bring a batch of cookies and an empty container, as well as enough copies of the recipe so everyone has one to take home.

When your guests arrive, mark each container with the type of cookie and the baker's name. Arrange the containers on a long table or counter.

Invite your guests to fill their empty containers, reminding them to take just as many cookies as they brought.

If you like, stir together this easy Chocolate Eggnog to serve with the cookies. Combine 1 quart (32 fluid-ounces) ready-to-drink NESTLÉ® QUIK® Chocolate Milk and 3 cups (24 fluid-ounces) prepared eggnog in a large pitcher or bowl. Chill. Sprinkle with ground nutmeg just before serving. Makes 8 to 10 servings.

just-for-kids cookie creations

lions and tigers and bears, oh yes! A little frosting turns cookies into whimsical zoo animals, spiderwebs or fanciful gingerbread people, which are sure to bring smiles and giggles. Gather the whole family to share in the cookie-baking fun, then offer a plateful of homemade cookies as reward.

Great Pumpkin Cookies (see recipe, page 122)

great pumpkin cookies

    2 cups all-purpose flour
1⅓ cups quick or old-fashioned oats
    1 teaspoon baking soda
    1 teaspoon ground cinnamon
  ½ teaspoon salt
    1 cup (2 sticks) butter or margarine, softened
    1 cup granulated sugar
    1 cup packed brown sugar
    1 cup LIBBY'S® Solid Pack Pumpkin
    1 egg
    1 teaspoon vanilla extract
  ¾ cup chopped nuts
  ¾ cup raisins
      Colored icings in tubes
      NESTLÉ® TOLL HOUSE® Semi-Sweet Chocolate Morsels
      Assorted candies

COMBINE flour, oats, baking soda, cinnamon and salt in medium bowl. Beat butter, granulated sugar and brown sugar in large mixer bowl until creamy. Beat in pumpkin, egg and vanilla extract until well mixed. Gradually beat in flour mixture. Stir in nuts and raisins. For *each* cookie, drop about ¼ *cup* dough onto greased baking sheet; spread dough into round, triangular or oval shapes about 3 inches across.

BAKE in preheated 350°F. oven for 14 to 16 minutes or until cookies are firm and lightly browned. Let stand for 2 minutes; remove to wire racks to cool completely. Decorate with icing, morsels and assorted candies. Makes about 20 large cookies.

Pictured on pages 120 and 121.

candy shop pizza

1 package (18 ounces) refrigerated NESTLÉ® TOLL HOUSE® Chocolate Chip Cookie Dough

1 cup (6 ounces) NESTLÉ® TOLL HOUSE® Semi-Sweet Chocolate Morsels

½ cup creamy or chunky peanut butter

1 cup coarsely chopped assorted candy: NESTLÉ® CRUNCH®, BUTTERFINGER®, BABY RUTH®, GOOBERS®, RAISINETS®

PRESS cookie dough evenly onto bottom of greased 12-inch pizza pan or 13 x 9-inch baking pan.

BAKE in preheated 350°F. oven for 14 to 18 minutes or until edge is set and center is still slightly soft. Immediately sprinkle morsels over hot crust; drop peanut butter by spoonfuls onto morsels. Let stand for 5 minutes or until morsels become shiny and soft. Gently spread chocolate and peanut butter evenly over cookie crust.

SPRINKLE candy in single layer over pizza. Cut into wedges; serve warm or at room temperature. Makes 12 servings.

Heading for the Kitchen

Although your children may be anxious to begin baking, things will go more smoothly if you take a few minutes to go over some basics. Make a game of rolling up sleeves, tying back long hair, washing hands and putting on an apron. Show your children how to use pot holders or hot pads for hot pans. Also, caution them never to set hot pans and utensils directly on the counter, but to place them on a hot pad or wire cooling rack instead. Finally, explain how to use scissors and knives safely. Now, you're ready to get on to the real fun—mixing up and baking delicious cookies.

just-for-kids cookie creations

spiderweb munch

2 cups (12-ounce package) NESTLÉ® TOLL HOUSE®
   Semi-Sweet Chocolate Morsels
1 cup creamy peanut butter, *divided*
⅓ cup powdered sugar
3 cups toasted rice cereal

HEAT morsels and ¾ *cup* peanut butter in small, *heavy-duty*
saucepan over low heat, stirring constantly until smooth; remove
from heat. Add powdered sugar; stir vigorously until smooth.

PLACE cereal in large bowl. Add 1 cup melted chocolate mixture;
stir until all cereal is coated. Place on ungreased baking sheet.
Using small metal spatula, shape into 10-inch circle with slightly
raised 1-inch-wide border. Pour remaining melted chocolate
mixture in center of circle; spread to border.

For Spiderweb:
PLACE *remaining* peanut butter in heavy-duty plastic bag. Cut
a small hole in corner of bag; squeeze to pipe peanut butter in
concentric circles on top of chocolate. Using wooden pick or tip
of sharp knife, pull tip through peanut butter from center to border.
Chill for 30 minutes or until firm. Cut into wedges to serve.
Makes 12 to 16 servings.

cookie pops

1⅔ cups all-purpose flour
1 teaspoon baking soda
½ teaspoon salt
1 cup (2 sticks) butter or margarine, softened
¾ cup granulated sugar
¾ cup packed brown sugar
2 teaspoons vanilla extract
2 eggs
2 cups (12-ounce package) NESTLÉ® TOLL HOUSE®
 Semi-Sweet Chocolate Morsels
2 cups quick or old-fashioned oats
1 cup raisins
 About 24 wooden craft sticks
1 container (16 ounces) prepared vanilla frosting, colored as
 desired
 Colored icing in tubes and/or colored candies

COMBINE flour, baking soda and salt in small bowl. Beat butter, granulated sugar, brown sugar and vanilla extract in large mixer bowl until creamy. Beat in eggs, one at a time, beating well after each addition. Gradually beat in flour mixture. Stir in morsels, oats and raisins. Drop dough by level ¼-cup measure about 3 inches apart onto ungreased baking sheets. Shape into rounded mounds. Insert wooden stick into side of each mound.

BAKE in preheated 325°F. oven for 14 to 18 minutes or until golden brown. Let stand for 2 minutes; remove to wire racks to cool completely. Decorate cookie pops using colored frosting and icing and/or candies. Makes about 2 dozen cookie pops.

Let the Kids in on the Fun!

Introducing kids to the delight of baking is not only a great indoor activity to keep them busy, but a way to teach skills they'll use throughout their lives. If you're looking for a fun, foolproof recipe for your first baking project, try Extra-Easy Cut-Out Cookies (see below).

Start by structuring the baking sessions so the children can do the "fun parts" without getting bored with the tedious tasks. For example, make doughs or frostings ahead so youngsters can jump right into cutting out cookies or frosting bars.

Tailor the children's involvement to suit their ages and interests. Young kids can roll dough into balls, push down on cookie cutters or sprinkle on simple toppings. Older children can assemble and mix batters or doughs, spread on frostings or position decorations. Pre-teens can do more involved tasks, such as sculpting dough, piping icing or preparing an entire recipe with minimal help.

To get started, involve your children by encouraging them to bake treats for special occasions. Allow them to choose what they'd like to make—for example, cutout snowmen or brownies. Then, choose recipes that are appropriate to their ability levels. Opt for simple recipes for preschoolers and save more elaborate ones for pre-teens.

Extra-Easy Cut-Out Cookies

The holidays wouldn't be the same without a batch of whimsically decorated cutout cookies. Short on time? No problem! Start with NESTLÉ® TOLL HOUSE® Refrigerated Sugar Cookie Dough and your favorite cookie cutters. These quick-fix cookies bake in just 6 to 9 minutes. To decorate the cooled cookies, use purchased or homemade vanilla frosting tinted with food coloring. For a thinner, glazelike topping, stir a small amount of light corn syrup into prepared frosting. Finish the cookies with your choice of candies or colored sugars.

giant decorated chocolate chip cookies

  2 cups all-purpose flour
  1 teaspoon baking soda
  ¼ teaspoon salt
1¼ cups packed brown sugar
  1 cup (2 sticks) butter or margarine, softened
  1 teaspoon vanilla extract
  1 egg
  2 cups (11½-ounce package) NESTLÉ® TOLL HOUSE® Milk
     Chocolate Morsels, *divided*
  1 cup chopped nuts
  1 cup raisins
  2 containers (16 ounces *each*) prepared vanilla frosting
     Colored icing in tubes
     Assorted candy

COMBINE flour, baking soda and salt in small bowl. Beat brown sugar, butter and vanilla extract in large mixer bowl until creamy. Beat in egg. Gradually beat in flour mixture. Stir in *1½ cups* morsels, nuts and raisins. Drop *½ cup* dough onto ungreased baking sheet; spread to 4-inch circle. Repeat with remaining dough.

BAKE in preheated 375°F. oven for 10 to 12 minutes or until edges are golden brown. Let stand for 5 minutes; remove to wire racks to cool completely.

DECORATE cookies with frosting, *remaining* morsels, icing and assorted candy, if desired. Makes 10 large cookies.

chocolate gingerbread boys and girls

2 cups (12-ounce package) NESTLÉ® TOLL HOUSE® Semi-Sweet Chocolate Morsels, *divided*

2¾ cups all-purpose flour

1 teaspoon baking soda

½ teaspoon salt

½ teaspoon ground ginger

½ teaspoon ground cinnamon

3 tablespoons butter or margarine, softened

3 tablespoons granulated sugar

½ cup molasses

¼ cup water

Prepared vanilla frosting or colored icing in tubes

MICROWAVE *1½ cups* morsels in medium, microwave-safe bowl on HIGH (100%) power for 1 minute; stir. Microwave at additional 10- to 20-second intervals, stirring until smooth. Cool to room temperature.

COMBINE flour, baking soda, salt, ginger and cinnamon in medium bowl. Beat butter and granulated sugar in small mixer bowl until creamy. Beat in molasses and melted chocolate. Gradually add flour mixture alternately with water, beating until smooth. Cover and chill for 1 hour or until firm.

ROLL *half* of dough to ¼-inch thickness on floured surface with floured rolling pin. Cut into gingerbread boys and girls, using cookie cutters or a stencil (see Cookie Creativity, *opposite page*). Place on ungreased baking sheets. Repeat with remaining dough.

BAKE in preheated 350°F. oven for 5 to 6 minutes or until edges are set but centers are still slightly soft. Let stand for 2 minutes; remove to wire racks to cool completely.

PLACE *remaining* morsels in heavy-duty plastic bag. Microwave on HIGH (100%) power for 45 seconds; knead. Microwave at additional 10-second intervals, kneading until smooth. Cut a small hole in corner of bag; squeeze to pipe over cookies. Decorate with piped frosting or icing. Makes 2½ dozen cookies.

just-for-kids cookie creations

chocolate marshmallow
mile-high squares

2 cups (12-ounce package) NESTLÉ® TOLL HOUSE®
   Semi-Sweet Chocolate Morsels

1⅔ cups (11-ounce package) NESTLÉ® TOLL HOUSE®
   Butterscotch Morsels

½ cup creamy or chunky peanut butter

9 cups (16-ounce package) miniature marshmallows

1 cup dry roasted peanuts

MICROWAVE semi-sweet morsels, butterscotch morsels and
peanut butter in large, microwave-safe bowl on MEDIUM-HIGH
(70%) power for 2 minutes; stir. Microwave at additional 10- to
20-second intervals, stirring until smooth. Cool for 1 minute. Stir
in marshmallows and nuts.

SPREAD into foil-lined 13 x 9-inch baking pan. Chill until firm.
Makes 48 squares.

Cookie Creativity

To add a playful touch to rolled cookies such as the Chocolate Gingerbread Boys
and Girls (opposite page), let your youngsters use any cookie cutters they like. Or,
cut a pattern out of heavy paper and lay it on your rolled-out cookie dough.
(The children can make simple drawings to use as patterns.) Use a knife to cut
carefully around the pattern.

tempting pies, tarts and cakes

pumpkin pie dates back to early Colonial America, but Libby's made it famous. This best-loved pie is one of the tempting recipes passed from generation to generation. Whether you're looking for a pie, tart, turnover, cake or cake roll recipe, these classics call for the same ingredients that our grandmas and moms used with wonderful results.

Libby's® Famous Pumpkin Pie (see recipe, page 134)

Libby's® famous pumpkin pie

1 unbaked 9-inch (4-cup volume) deep-dish pie shell (see recipe, *page 154*) or two shallow unbaked 9-inch (2-cup volume) pie shells

¾ cup granulated sugar

1 teaspoon ground cinnamon

½ teaspoon salt

½ teaspoon ground ginger

¼ teaspoon ground cloves

2 eggs

1¾ cups (15-ounce can) LIBBY'S® Solid Pack Pumpkin

1½ cups (12 fluid-ounce can) NESTLÉ® CARNATION® Evaporated Milk

Whipped cream (optional)

Chopped nuts (optional)

COMBINE sugar, cinnamon, salt, ginger and cloves in small bowl. Beat eggs lightly in large bowl. Stir in pumpkin and sugar mixture. Gradually stir in evaporated milk. Pour into pie shell(s).

BAKE* in preheated 425°F. oven 15 minutes. Reduce temperature to 350°F. Bake 40 to 50 minutes more for one 4-cup volume pie (15 to 20 minutes for 2 shallow pies) or until knife inserted near center comes out clean. Cool on wire rack(s). Garnish with whipped cream and nuts, if desired. Makes 1 or 2 pies (8 servings each).

*Note: If using a metal or foil pan(s), bake on preheated, *heavy-duty* baking sheet.

Pictured on pages 132 and 133.

Use a wire whisk or fork to beat the eggs lightly in a large bowl. Add the pumpkin and sugar mixture and stir together.

Pour the pumpkin mixture into the prepared pie shell, being careful not to drip any of the pumpkin mixture on the edge of the pie shell.

To test for doneness, insert a knife near the center. If it comes out clean, the pie is done. If some of the pumpkin mixture clings to the knife, bake the pie a few more minutes.

lighter Libby's®
famous pumpkin pie

Lower Fat

1 unbaked 9-inch (4-cup volume) deep-dish pie shell (see recipe, *page 154*) or two shallow unbaked 9-inch (2-cup volume) pie shells

¾ cup granulated sugar

1 tablespoon cornstarch

1 teaspoon ground cinnamon

½ teaspoon salt

½ teaspoon ground ginger

2 egg whites

1¾ cups (15-ounce can) LIBBY'S® Solid Pack Pumpkin

1½ cups (12 fluid-ounce can) NESTLÉ® CARNATION® Evaporated Skimmed Milk

COMBINE sugar, cornstarch, cinnamon, salt and ginger in small bowl. Beat egg whites lightly in large bowl. Stir in pumpkin and sugar mixture. Gradually stir in evaporated skimmed milk. Pour into pie shell(s).

BAKE* in preheated 425°F. oven for 15 minutes. Reduce oven temperature to 350°F. Bake for 30 to 40 minutes more for one 4-cup volume pie (15 to 20 minutes for 2 shallow pies) or until knife inserted near center comes out clean. Cool pie(s) on wire rack(s). Makes 1 or 2 pies (8 servings each). Per serving (4-cup volume pie): 5 grams fat and 210 calories.

*Note: If using a metal or foil pan(s), bake on preheated, *heavy-duty* baking sheet.

pumpkin pecan pie

PUMPKIN LAYER

- 1 unbaked 9-inch (4-cup volume) deep-dish pie shell (see recipe, *page 154*)
- 1 egg
- 1 cup LIBBY'S® Solid Pack Pumpkin
- ⅓ cup granulated sugar
- 1 teaspoon pumpkin pie spice

PECAN LAYER

- ⅔ cup light corn syrup
- 2 eggs
- ½ cup granulated sugar
- 3 tablespoons butter or margarine, melted
- ½ teaspoon vanilla extract
- 1 cup pecan halves
  Vanilla ice cream (optional)

For Pumpkin Layer:
COMBINE egg, pumpkin, sugar and pumpkin pie spice in medium bowl. Spread over bottom of pie shell.

For Pecan Layer:
COMBINE corn syrup, eggs, sugar, butter and vanilla extract in medium bowl; stir in pecans. Spoon over pumpkin layer.

BAKE* in preheated 350°F. oven for 50 minutes or until filling is set. Cool on wire rack. Serve with ice cream. Makes 8 servings.

*Note: If using a metal or foil pan, bake on preheated, *heavy-duty* baking sheet.

Libby's® Pumpkin Brings Pure Pleasure

Since 1929, people who love to bake have enjoyed the convenience, rich flavor and perfect texture of Libby's® Solid Pack Pumpkin. Year after year, they've relied on this all-natural product to bring out the best in their favorite recipes.

At Libby's, not just any pumpkin will do. After years of research, Libby's developed its own superior breed of the Dickinson pumpkin. Called the Libby's Select, this sweet and meaty pumpkin boasts plenty of flavor, less water and a rich, golden color. This product ensures moist, sweet- and fresh-tasting results time after time.

peanut butter pumpkin pie

    1 unbaked 9-inch (4-cup volume) deep-dish pie shell
        (see recipe, *page 154*)
1¾ cups (15-ounce can) LIBBY'S® Solid Pack Pumpkin
    1 cup NESTLÉ® CARNATION® Evaporated Milk
    ¾ cup packed brown sugar
    3 eggs
    ½ cup creamy peanut butter
    ½ teaspoon pumpkin pie spice
    ¼ teaspoon salt
        Whipped cream (optional)
        Chopped peanuts (optional)

COMBINE pumpkin, evaporated milk, brown sugar, eggs, peanut butter, pumpkin pie spice and salt in large bowl. Pour into pie shell.

BAKE* in preheated 425°F. oven for 15 minutes. Reduce temperature to 350°F.; bake for 40 to 45 minutes more or until knife inserted near center comes out clean. Cool on wire rack. Garnish with whipped cream and peanuts. Makes 8 servings.

*Note: If using a metal or foil pan, bake on preheated, *heavy-duty* baking sheet.

Pie-Making Perfection

In the years since 1950 when Libby's® Famous Pumpkin Pie (see recipe, page 134) first appeared on the Libby's canned pumpkin label, this delectable pie has become an American tradition. With more than 55 million Libby's pumpkin pies made each year, it is no surprise that bakers turn to Libby's for advice. Remember these tips for easy-as-pie success:

For custard-type pies that call for eggs and milk, use a wire whisk to thoroughly mix the filling ingredients.

When baking pumpkin and other custard-type pies, start with the higher temperature to help "set" the crust, preventing it from getting soggy. Switch to the lower temperature, allowing the pie to bake gradually and prevent it from burning. Also, make sure your oven rack is centered in the oven (no higher) to avoid a crust from forming on the top of your pie.

Use a glass or dull-finished aluminum pan for a crisper bottom crust. If you use a shiny aluminum or foil pan, bake the pie on a preheated heavy-duty baking sheet.

Bake pies one at a time for more even baking. If you need to bake two pies at a time, place them on separate racks; switch and rotate the pies halfway through baking time.

If the edge of the crust starts to brown too quickly, cut a 9-inch circle from the center of a square piece of aluminum foil. Carefully place the square piece over the edge of the crust and continue baking until the pie is done.

To determine if a pumpkin pie is done, insert a knife near the center of the pie (about 1 to 1½ inches from the center). If the knife comes out clean with no custard filling clinging to it, the pie is done. Overbaking can cause a pie to crack or pull away from the crust.

You can't freeze pumpkin pie, but you can freeze the filling and pie crust separately (for up to one month). Thaw, stir and pour the filling into the crust, baking as directed. Thaw the crust, too, if prepared in a glass pie plate. Crusts prepared in metal or aluminum pans do not need thawing.

Libby's® super-quick pumpkin pie

1 unbaked 9-inch (4-cup volume) deep-dish pie shell (see recipe, *page 154*) or two shallow unbaked 9-inch (2-cup volume) pie shells

2 eggs

3¼ cups (30-ounce can) LIBBY'S® Pumpkin Pie Mix

⅔ cup NESTLÉ® CARNATION® Evaporated Milk

BEAT eggs lightly in large bowl. Stir in pumpkin pie mix and evaporated milk. Pour into pie shell(s).

BAKE* in preheated 425°F. oven 15 minutes. Reduce temperature to 350°F. Bake 50 to 60 minutes more for one 4-cup volume pie (about 30 minutes for 2 shallow pies) or until knife inserted near center comes out clean. Cool on wire rack(s). Makes 1 or 2 pies (8 servings each).

*Note: If using a metal or foil pan(s), bake on preheated, *heavy-duty* baking sheet.

Whipped Cream Any Way You Like It

Add a touch of elegance to your favorite pie or dessert with a dollop of sweetened whipped cream. To make 2 cups, combine 1 cup heavy whipping cream, 2 tablespoons sugar and ½ teaspoon vanilla extract in a chilled bowl. Beat with chilled beaters of an electric mixer on medium speed until soft peaks form.

For extra flavor, add one of the following with the vanilla extract: 2 tablespoons orange-flavored liqueur, 1 teaspoon NESCAFÉ® Expresso Roast, ½ teaspoon finely shredded orange peel or ¼ teaspoon ground cinnamon or nutmeg.

To save some whipped cream for later, spoon any extra whipped cream into mounds on a waxed paper-lined baking sheet. Freeze until firm. Transfer the frozen mounds to a container; seal, label and freeze for up to one month. To serve, let the mounds stand at room temperature for 5 minutes.

frozen cranberry orange pumpkin pie

CRUST
1 cup plus 2 tablespoons graham cracker crumbs
3 tablespoons butter or margarine, melted
2 tablespoons granulated sugar

FILLING
2 cups (1 pint) orange sherbet, softened
1 cup LIBBY'S® Solid Pack Pumpkin
¼ cup chopped cranberries
1 cup (½ pint) vanilla low-fat or nonfat
   frozen yogurt
½ teaspoon grated orange peel

For Crust:
COMBINE graham cracker crumbs, butter and sugar in medium bowl. Press crumbs onto bottom and up side of 9-inch pie plate. Bake in preheated 375°F. oven for 6 minutes. Cool on wire rack.

For Filling:
COMBINE sherbet, pumpkin and cranberries in medium bowl. Spread evenly over crust; freeze for 2 hours.

SOFTEN frozen yogurt in small bowl. Add orange peel; mix well. Spread mixture over pie; freeze for 2 hours. Makes 8 servings. Per serving: 6 grams fat and 220 calories.

pumpkin almond pie

CRUST
- 1 cup all-purpose flour
- ¼ cup slivered almonds, toasted and finely chopped
- ½ teaspoon salt
- ½ cup shortening
- 2 to 3 tablespoons cold water

PUMPKIN LAYER
- 1 egg
- 1 cup LIBBY'S® Solid Pack Pumpkin
- ⅓ cup granulated sugar
- 1 teaspoon pumpkin pie spice

ALMOND LAYER
- ⅔ cup light corn syrup
- 2 eggs
- ½ cup granulated sugar
- 3 tablespoons butter or margarine, melted
- ½ teaspoon almond extract
- 1 cup slivered almonds, toasted

For Crust:
COMBINE flour, almonds and salt in medium bowl; cut in shortening with pastry blender or 2 knives until mixture resembles coarse crumbs. Gradually add water, mixing until ball forms. On lightly floured surface, roll into 12-inch circle. Fit into 9-inch pie plate. Turn under edge; flute.

For Pumpkin Layer:
COMBINE egg, pumpkin, sugar and pumpkin pie spice in medium bowl. Spread over bottom of the pie shell.

For Almond Layer:
COMBINE corn syrup, eggs, sugar, butter and almond extract in medium bowl; stir in almonds. Spoon over pumpkin layer.

BAKE in preheated 350°F. oven for 50 to 55 minutes or until filling is set. Cool on wire rack. Makes 8 servings.

pumpkin mousse ice-cream pie

1 1/4 cups crushed gingersnap cookies (about 28 cookies)
1/3 cup butter, melted
1 cup granulated sugar, *divided*
2 cups (1 pint) vanilla ice cream
1 cup LIBBY'S® Solid Pack Pumpkin
1 1/2 teaspoons pumkin pie spice
1 cup (8-ounce carton) whipping cream
1/2 teaspoon vanilla extract
Pumpkin Topping (recipe follows)

COMBINE crushed gingersnap cookies, butter and 1/4 *cup* sugar in small bowl. Press onto bottom and side of 9-inch pie plate. Bake in preheated 375°F. oven for 8 minutes. Cool on wire rack. Soften ice cream; spread over crust. Freeze until firm.

COMBINE pumpkin, *remaining* sugar and pumpkin pie spice in medium bowl. Beat whipping cream and vanilla extract in small mixer bowl until stiff; fold into pumpkin mixture. Spoon over ice cream. Freeze until firm. Serve with Pumpkin Topping. Makes 8 servings.

For Pumpkin Topping:
COMBINE 1 jar (12 1/4 ounces) caramel- or butterscotch-flavored ice-cream topping, 1/2 cup LIBBY'S® Solid Pack Pumpkin and 1/2 teaspoon pumpkin pie spice in small bowl.

sour cream orange pumpkin pie

1 unbaked 9-inch (4-cup volume) deep-dish pie shell (see recipe, *page 154*)
2 eggs
1¾ cups (15-ounce can) LIBBY'S® Solid Pack Pumpkin
1¼ cups (14-ounce can) NESTLÉ® CARNATION® Sweetened Condensed Milk
1 tablespoon pumpkin pie spice
2 teaspoons grated orange peel
½ teaspoon salt
Sour Cream Orange Topping (recipe follows)
Orange slices, cut into wedges (optional)

COMBINE eggs, pumpkin, sweetened condensed milk, pumpkin pie spice, orange peel and salt in medium bowl; mix well. Pour into prepared pie shell.

BAKE in preheated 425°F. oven for 15 minutes. Reduce temperature to 350°F.; bake for 30 to 35 minutes or until knife inserted near center comes out clean. Cool pie for 10 minutes on wire rack.

SPREAD with Sour Cream Orange Topping; bake at 350°F. for 8 minutes. Cool on wire rack. Garnish with orange wedges. Makes 8 servings.

For Sour Cream Orange Topping:
COMBINE 1¼ cups sour cream, 2 tablespoons granulated sugar, 2 teaspoons thawed frozen orange juice concentrate (or orange-flavored liqueur) and ½ teaspoon grated orange peel in small bowl.

*Note: If using a metal or foil pan, bake on preheated, *heavy-duty* baking sheet.

Sour Cream Orange Pumpkin Pie (see recipe above) and
Pumpkin Cheesecake Tarts (see recipe, page 161)

walnut crunch pumpkin pie

1 unbaked 9-inch (4-cup volume) deep-dish pie shell (see recipe, *page 154*)
1¼ cups coarsely chopped walnuts
¾ cup packed brown sugar
1¾ cups (15-ounce can) LIBBY'S® Solid Pack Pumpkin
1½ cups (12 fluid-ounce can) NESTLÉ® CARNATION® Evaporated Milk
¾ cup granulated sugar
2 eggs
1 teaspoon ground cinnamon
¾ teaspoon ground ginger
¼ teaspoon salt
¼ teaspoon ground cloves
3 tablespoons butter, melted

MIX walnuts and brown sugar in small bowl; place ¾ *cup* in bottom of pie shell. Reserve remaining mixture for topping. Combine pumpkin, evaporated milk, granulated sugar, eggs, cinnamon, ginger, salt and cloves in large bowl; mix well. Pour into pie shell.

BAKE* in preheated 425°F. oven for 15 minutes. Reduce temperature to 350°F.; bake for 40 to 50 minutes more or until knife inserted near center comes out clean. Cool on wire rack.

ADD butter to *remaining* nut-sugar mixture; stir until moistened. Sprinkle over cooled pie. Broil about 5 inches from heat for 2 to 3 minutes or until bubbly. Cool on wire rack. Makes 8 servings.

*Note: If using a metal or foil pan, bake on preheated, *heavy-duty* baking sheet.

pumpkin apricot crumble pie

1 unbaked 9-inch (4-cup volume) deep-dish pie shell
  (see recipe, *page 154*)
¾ cup finely chopped dried apricots
¾ cup coarsely chopped walnuts
¾ cup packed brown sugar
1¾ cups (15-ounce can) LIBBY'S® Solid Pack Pumpkin
1¼ cups NESTLÉ® CARNATION® Evaporated Milk
2 eggs
½ cup granulated sugar
¼ cup apricot preserves
1 teaspoon ground cinnamon
1 teaspoon ground ginger
¼ teaspoon salt
¼ teaspoon ground cloves
3 tablespoons butter, melted

MIX apricots, walnuts and brown sugar in small bowl; place ¾ *cup* in bottom of pie shell. Reserve remaining mixture for topping. Combine pumpkin, evaporated milk, eggs, granulated sugar, apricot preserves, cinnamon, ginger, salt and cloves in large bowl; mix well. Pour into pie shell.

BAKE* in preheated 425°F. oven for 15 minutes. Reduce temperature to 350°F.; bake for 40 to 50 minutes more or until knife inserted near center comes out clean. Cool on wire rack.

ADD butter to *remaining* apricot mixture; stir until moistened. Sprinkle over cooled pie. Broil about 5 inches from heat for 2 to 3 minutes or until bubbly. Cool on wire rack. Makes 8 servings.

*Note: If using a metal or foil pan, bake on preheated, *heavy-duty* baking sheet.

pumpkin dutch apple pie

APPLE LAYER

- 1 unbaked 9-inch (4-cup volume) pie shell with high fluted edge (see recipe, *page 154*)
- 2 medium-size green apples, peeled and thinly sliced (about 2 cups)
- ¼ cup granulated sugar
- 2 teaspoons all-purpose flour
- 1 teaspoon lemon juice
- ¼ teaspoon ground cinnamon

PUMPKIN LAYER

- 2 eggs
- 1½ cups LIBBY'S® Solid Pack Pumpkin
- 1 cup NESTLÉ® CARNATION® Evaporated Milk
- ½ cup granulated sugar
- 2 tablespoons butter or margarine, melted
- ¾ teaspoon ground cinnamon
- ¼ teaspoon salt
- ⅛ teaspoon ground nutmeg
  Crumble Topping (recipe follows)

For Apple Layer:
COMBINE apples with sugar, flour, lemon juice and cinnamon in medium bowl; place in pie shell.

For Pumpkin Layer:
COMBINE eggs, pumpkin, evaporated milk, sugar, butter, cinnamon, salt and nutmeg in medium bowl; pour over apples.

BAKE in preheated 375°F. oven for 30 minutes. Remove from oven; sprinkle with Crumble Topping. Bake for 20 minutes more or until custard is set. Cool on wire rack. Makes 8 servings.

For Crumble Topping:
COMBINE ½ cup all-purpose flour, ⅓ cup chopped walnuts and 5 tablespoons granulated sugar in medium bowl. Cut in 3 tablespoons softened butter with pastry blender or 2 knives until crumbly.

What to Do with Extra Pumpkin

If your recipe calls for less than a whole can of pumpkin (approximately 1¾ cups), save the rest and try one of the quick-fix ideas below. Before storing, always transfer the pumpkin from the can to an airtight container or zip-top plastic bag. Store leftover pumpkin in the refrigerator for 1 week or in the freezer for up to 3 months.

Stir pumpkin into softened ice cream (try vanilla, caramel swirl or butter pecan flavors) for a quick, new dessert idea.

Mix pumpkin with prepared (and partially set-up) vanilla or butterscotch pudding. For a fast and easy fat-free treat, use fat-free pudding made with nonfat milk and pumpkin.

Whisk pumpkin into soups and sauces. You'll add flavor and nutrients.

Stir pumpkin into mashed potatoes for a festive, fall-color favorite.

Special Finishing Touches

A dusting of powdered sugar or a sprinkling of nuts can turn the most basic dessert into a showpiece. Count on these simple garnishing ideas to dress up your pies, cakes and other baked goods.

Edible flowers, including nasturtiums, pansies and violets, offer simple elegance atop desserts or on dessert plates. Look for edible flowers in supermarkets or local gardens. Make sure they are chemical-free.

Turn to the fruit bowl for fresh and simple garnishes. Strawberry fans, thinly sliced citrus, assorted berries and kiwi fruit wedges add bursts of color and flavor, too.

For easy drizzling with no mess, create a makeshift pastry bag from a heavy-duty zip-top plastic bag. To drizzle chocolate, snip a small hole in a corner of a bag filled with melted NESTLÉ® TOLL HOUSE® Morsels (see Masterful Melting, page 234). Use to write, design or draw, decorating desserts or plates in your own creative way. This makeshift pastry bag works well for icing and jelly designs, too.

Press handfuls of chopped nuts along the sides of a frosted cake or sprinkle them on top. Whole nuts, caramelized nuts and chocolate-dipped nuts also jazz up desserts.

Add the look of lace or a stenciled design atop cakes with doilies or stencils. Lay the doily or stencil atop the cake and gently sift powdered sugar or unsweetened cocoa over the top. Carefully remove the doily or stencil to see your work of art. For a striped or checkerboard design, position strips of waxed paper on the cake and repeat as above.

luscious chocolate mousse pie

1   8-inch (6 ounces) prepared chocolate crumb crust
2¼ cups (about 13.5 ounces) NESTLÉ® TOLL HOUSE® Semi-
     Sweet Chocolate Morsels, *divided*
2   cups heavy whipping cream, *divided*
2   teaspoons powdered sugar
1   teaspoon vanilla extract
     Chocolate Drizzle (recipe follows)

MICROWAVE *2 cups* morsels and *¾ cup* cream in large,
microwave-safe bowl on HIGH (100%) power for 1 minute; stir.
Microwave at additional 10- to 20-second intervals, stirring until
smooth; cool to room temperature.

BEAT *remaining* cream, powdered sugar and vanilla extract in
chilled small mixer bowl until soft peaks form. Fold 2 cups whipped
cream into chocolate mixture. Spoon into crust; swirl top. Garnish
with remaining whipped cream; chill until firm. Garnish with
Chocolate Drizzle; let stand a few minutes before serving.
Makes 8 servings.

For Chocolate Drizzle:
PLACE *remaining* morsels in heavy-duty plastic bag. Microwave on
HIGH (100%) power about 30 seconds; knead until smooth. Cut a
small hole in corner of bag; squeeze to drizzle chocolate over pie.

pumpkin turnovers

PASTRY
2½ cups all-purpose flour

2 tablespoons granulated sugar

1 teaspoon salt

½ teaspoon ground cinnamon

½ cup (1 stick) butter or margarine, melted

½ cup milk

1 egg

FILLING
1¾ cups (15-ounce can) LIBBY'S® Solid Pack Pumpkin

¾ cup packed brown sugar

¾ cup chopped pecans or walnuts

½ cup raisins

1 tablespoon lemon juice

1 tablespoon water

1 teaspoon ground cinnamon

⅛ teaspoon ground cloves

1 egg, lightly beaten
Cinnamon Sugar (recipe follows)

For Pastry:
COMBINE flour, granulated sugar, salt and cinnamon in medium bowl. Beat butter, milk and egg in small bowl until combined. Add to flour mixture; mix well. Form into ball. Cover; chill for 1 hour.

For Filling:
COMBINE pumpkin and brown sugar in medium bowl. Add pecans, raisins, lemon juice, water, cinnamon and cloves; mix well.

DIVIDE pastry into 12 to 14 portions. On lightly floured board, roll *each* portion into 6-inch circle. Place *scant* ¼ *cup* filling on each circle. Moisten edges with water; fold in half, pressing edges with fork to seal. Scallop sealed edges by indenting with handle of fork at ¾-inch intervals. Place on ungreased baking sheet. Brush egg over tops of turnovers. Sprinkle with Cinnamon Sugar.

BAKE in preheated 400°F. oven for 15 to 20 minutes or until golden brown. Serve warm, or cool on wire rack. Makes 12 to 14.

For Cinnamon Sugar:
COMBINE ¼ cup granulated sugar and 1 teaspoon ground cinnamon in small bowl.

homemade pastry

1 cup all-purpose flour
½ teaspoon salt
6 tablespoons shortening
2 to 3 tablespoons cold water

MIX flour and salt in medium bowl; cut in shortening with pastry blender or 2 knives until crumbly (see photo, *below left*). Gradually stir in cold water, mixing until flour is moistened.

SHAPE dough into ball; flatten to 1-inch thickness. On lightly floured board, roll dough into a circle about 2 inches larger than inverted 9-inch pie plate. Line pie plate with pastry (see photo, *below center*). Trim pastry to ½ inch beyond the edge of the pie plate; fold extra pastry under and flute edge (see photo, *below right*). Makes one 9-inch pie crust.

Note: Recipe can be doubled to make two 9-inch pie crusts or one double-crust 9-inch pie.

Use a pastry blender or 2 knives to cut in the shortening until mixture is crumbly.

Ease pastry into pie plate, being careful not to stretch pastry.

Trim pastry to ½ inch beyond edge of pie plate, fold under and flute edges.

Secrets to Pastry Success

The first step to exceptional pies is tender, flaky pie crust. For perfect pastry you can brag about, follow this pie crust advice.

Measure the ingredients carefully. Too much flour makes the finished pie crust tough; too much shortening makes it crumbly.

Use a pastry blender or 2 knives to cut in the shortening so it is distributed evenly in the flour mixture and the mixture is crumbly.

Add the cold water gradually to the flour-shortening mixture and toss it together until the mixture is moistened evenly. Don't add too much water or your crust will be soggy or tough.

When it's time to roll out the crust, use as little flour as possible and roll the pastry to an even thickness. Adding too much flour at this step will make the crust tough, and a crust of uneven thickness will shrink excessively.

To transfer the pastry to the pie plate quickly and easily, wrap it around the rolling pin. Then, starting at one side of the pie plate, unroll the pastry into the plate. To avoid shrinkage of the crust as it bakes, don't stretch the pastry as you ease it into the plate (see photo, opposite page).

Patch any cracks with a pastry scrap before adding the filling. Moisten the underside of the scrap with a little water so it stays in place.

Trim the pastry ½ inch beyond the rim of the pie plate and fold it under to build up the edge. For a fluted edge (see photo, opposite page), place your index finger against the outside of the pastry; press the dough around your finger with your other hand's thumb and index finger.

Check that your oven temperature is accurate. If it is too low, the crust will be soggy. If it's too high, the pie won't bake evenly.

After baking, cool the pie on a wire rack. Allowing air to circulate under the pie as it cools keeps the pastry from becoming soggy.

If you don't have time to make pie pastry from scratch, use refrigerated pie crust, unbaked frozen pastry shells or pastry made from a pie crust mix instead of homemade pastry.

macadamia cheesecake tart

CRUST

- 1 cup chopped macadamia nuts
- 1 cup quick or old-fashioned oats
- 1 cup flaked coconut
- 2 tablespoons granulated sugar
- 7 tablespoons butter

FILLING

- 1 package (8 ounces) cream cheese, softened
- ½ cup granulated sugar
- 2 eggs
- 1¾ cups (15-ounce can) LIBBY'S® Solid Pack Pumpkin
- 2 teaspoons ground cinnamon
- 1 teaspoon ground ginger
- 1 teaspoon vanilla extract

  Chopped macadamia nuts (optional)

  Toasted coconut (optional)

For Crust:

COMBINE macadamia nuts, oats, coconut and sugar in medium bowl. Cut in butter with pastry blender or 2 knives until blended. Press dough evenly onto bottom and up sides of 11-inch tart pan with removable bottom. Bake in preheated 350°F. oven for 20 to 25 minutes or until lightly browned.

For Filling:

BEAT cream cheese and sugar in large mixer bowl until well blended. Add eggs, pumpkin, cinnamon, ginger and vanilla extract; blend well. Pour into baked crust.

BAKE at 350°F. for 35 to 40 minutes or until knife inserted near center comes out clean. Cool on wire rack. Chill. Remove side of tart pan. Garnish with additional macadamia nuts and coconut. Makes 14 servings.

crumb-topped pumpkin pear tart

PEAR LAYER

Pastry for single crust (see recipe, *page 154*)

2 medium-size pears, peeled and thinly sliced (about 2 cups)

2 tablespoons granulated sugar

2 teaspoons all-purpose flour

¼ teaspoon ground cinnamon

PUMPKIN LAYER

2 eggs

1½ cups LIBBY'S® Solid Pack Pumpkin

1 cup NESTLÉ® CARNATION® Evaporated Milk

½ cup granulated sugar

2 tablespoons butter or margarine, melted

¾ teaspoon ground cinnamon

¼ teaspoon salt

⅛ teaspoon ground nutmeg
Crumb Topping (recipe follows)

For Pear Layer:
PLACE pastry in a 10- or 11-inch tart pan with removable bottom (or a 9-inch pie plate). Trim excess pastry.* Combine pears with sugar, flour and cinnamon in medium bowl; place in tart shell.

For Pumpkin Layer:
COMBINE eggs, pumpkin, evaporated milk, sugar, butter, cinnamon, salt and nutmeg in bowl; pour mixture over pears. Bake in preheated 375°F. oven 25 minutes (30 minutes for pie plate). Remove from oven; sprinkle with Crumb Topping. Bake tart 15 minutes more (20 minutes for pie plate) or until custard is set. Cool. Remove side of tart pan. Makes 10 servings.

For Crumb Topping:
COMBINE ½ cup all-purpose flour, ⅓ cup chopped walnuts and 5 tablespoons granulated sugar in medium bowl. Cut in 3 tablespoons softened butter or margarine with pastry blender or 2 knives until crumbly.

*Note: If desired, cut pastry scraps into decorative designs; place on an ungreased baking sheet. Brush with beaten egg. Bake in 375°F. oven 10 minutes or until golden. Place atop baked tart.

chocolate chip fruit tart

1 package (18 ounces) refrigerated NESTLÉ® TOLL HOUSE® Chocolate Chip Cookie Dough
1 package (8 ounces) cream cheese, softened
⅓ cup granulated sugar
½ teaspoon vanilla extract
1½ cups fruit (raspberries or blueberries and/or sliced kiwi, bananas, peaches or strawberries)

PRESS dough evenly into bottom and up sides of greased 9-inch fluted tart pan with removable bottom.*

BAKE in preheated 350°F. oven for 18 to 20 minutes or until edge is set and center is still slightly soft. Cool completely in pan on wire rack.

BEAT cream cheese, sugar and vanilla extract in small mixer bowl until smooth. Spread evenly over cooled cookie crust to within ½ inch of edge; arrange fruit as desired. Chill for 1 hour. Remove side of tart pan; slice into wedges. Makes 8 to 10 servings.

*Note: If tart pan is not available, press cookie dough onto greased baking sheet into a 9- to 10-inch circle. Bake for 14 to 18 minutes.

pumpkin cheesecake tarts

⅔ cup finely crushed gingersnap cookies
  (about 12 cookies)
2 tablespoons butter or margarine, melted
1 package (8 ounces) cream cheese, softened
1 cup LIBBY'S® Solid Pack Pumpkin
½ cup granulated sugar
1 teaspoon pumpkin pie spice
1 teaspoon vanilla extract
2 eggs
2 tablespoons sour cream (optional)
2 tablespoons NESTLÉ® TOLL HOUSE® Semi-Sweet Chocolate
  Morsels (optional)

COMBINE crushed gingersnap cookies and butter in small bowl.
Press *scant tablespoon* cookie mixture onto bottom of *each* of
12 paper-lined muffin cups. Bake in preheated 325°F. oven
for 5 minutes.

BEAT cream cheese, pumpkin, sugar, pumpkin pie spice and
vanilla extract in small mixer bowl until blended. Add eggs; beat
well. Pour into muffin cups, filling ¾ full.

BAKE at 325°F. for 25 to 30 minutes or until set. Cool in pan on
wire rack. Remove tarts from pan; chill.

GARNISH with sour cream. Place morsels in small, heavy-duty
plastic bag. Microwave on HIGH (100%) power for 20 seconds;
knead bag to mix. Microwave at additional 10-second intervals,
kneading until smooth. Cut a small hole in corner of bag; squeeze
to drizzle chocolate over tarts. Makes 1 dozen tarts.

Pictured on page 144.

pumpkin meringue tarts

MERINGUE TARTS

3 egg whites

½ teaspoon cream of tartar

¼ teaspoon salt

¾ cup granulated sugar

Ground cinnamon (optional)

FILLING

1 package (4-serving size) instant sugar-free vanilla pudding

1½ cups low-fat or nonfat milk

1 cup LIBBY'S® Solid Pack Pumpkin

1 teaspoon ground cinnamon

For Meringue Tarts:
BEAT egg whites, cream of tartar and salt in small mixer bowl on high speed until soft peaks form. Gradually add sugar, beating on high speed until stiff peaks form (see photo, *page 102*). Spoon mixture onto lightly greased baking sheets (or use pastry bag with star tip), forming eight round or oval 4-inch "nests."

BAKE in preheated 300°F. oven for 30 to 35 minutes or until crisp. Cool on baking sheets for 5 minutes; remove to wire racks to cool completely. Sprinkle lightly with ground cinnamon, if desired.

For Filling:
BEAT pudding and milk according to package directions; chill for 5 minutes. Add pumpkin and 1 teaspoon cinnamon; mix well. Chill for 10 minutes. Spoon filling (or use pastry bag with star tip) into meringue tarts. Serve immediately. Makes 8 tarts. Per tart: 1 gram fat and 140 calories.

pumpkin carrot cake

2 cups all-purpose flour
2 teaspoons baking soda
2 teaspoons ground cinnamon
½ teaspoon salt
¾ cup milk
1½ teaspoons lemon juice
1½ cups granulated sugar
1¼ cups LIBBY'S® Solid Pack Pumpkin
3 eggs

½ cup packed brown sugar
½ cup vegetable oil
1 cup (8-ounce can) crushed pineapple, drained
1 cup grated carrots (about 3 medium)
1 cup flaked coconut
1¼ cups chopped walnuts, *divided*
Cream Cheese Frosting (recipe follows)

COMBINE flour, baking soda, cinnamon and salt in small bowl. Combine milk and lemon juice in liquid measuring cup (mixture will appear curdled).

BEAT granulated sugar, pumpkin, eggs, brown sugar and vegetable oil in large mixer bowl until combined. Beat in pineapple, carrots and milk mixture until combined. Gradually beat in flour mixture. Stir in coconut and *1 cup* walnuts. Pour into 2 greased 9-inch round cake pans.

BAKE in preheated 350°F. oven for 30 to 35 minutes or until wooden pick inserted in center comes out clean. Cool in pans on wire racks for 15 minutes. Remove to racks to cool completely.

To Assemble:
FROST between layers, on side and top of cake with Cream Cheese Frosting. Garnish side of cake with *remaining* walnuts. Store in refrigerator. Makes 12 servings.

For Cream Cheese Frosting:
BEAT 1 package (8 ounces) *and* 1 package (3 ounces) softened cream cheese and ⅓ cup softened butter in large mixer bowl; gradually beat in 3½ cups sifted powdered sugar. Beat in 2 teaspoons orange juice, 1 teaspoon vanilla extract and 1 teaspoon grated orange peel until fluffy.

pumpkin crunch cake

1   package (18¼ ounces) yellow cake mix, *divided*
1⅔ cups LIBBY'S® Pumpkin Pie Mix
2   eggs
2   teaspoons pumpkin pie spice
⅓   cup flaked coconut
¼   cup chopped nuts
3   tablespoons butter or margarine, softened

COMBINE *3 cups* dry cake mix, pumpkin pie mix, eggs and pumpkin pie spice in large mixer bowl until moistened. Beat on medium speed for 2 minutes. Spread batter into greased 13 x 9-inch baking pan.

COMBINE *remaining* dry cake mix, coconut and nuts in small bowl; cut in butter with pastry blender or 2 knives until crumbly. Sprinkle mixture over batter.

BAKE in preheated 350°F. oven for 30 to 35 minutes or until wooden pick inserted in center comes out clean. Cool in pan on wire rack. Makes 20 servings.

Grease It Right

To grease cake pans just enough, but not too much, spread on the shortening with a paper towel and use about 1 teaspoon for an 8- or 9-inch round cake pan and 1½ to 2 teaspoons for a 13 x 9-inch baking pan or a 15 x 10-inch jelly-roll pan. If you want to leave the cake in the pan for serving, grease only the bottom. If you plan to remove the cake from the pan, grease and flour both the bottom and sides of the pan. To flour a pan, sprinkle a little flour into the pan once you've greased it. Then, tilt and tap the pan so the flour covers all the greased surfaces. Tap out any excess flour.

pumpkin
white chunk cake

3 cups buttermilk baking mix

1½ cups granulated sugar

2½ teaspoons ground cinnamon

1 cup LIBBY'S® Solid Pack Pumpkin

2 eggs, lightly beaten

½ cup water

2 teaspoons vanilla extract

3 bars (one 6-ounce package) NESTLÉ® TOLL HOUSE® Premier White Baking Bars, coarsely chopped, *divided*

⅔ cup chopped pecans, *divided*

STIR together baking mix, sugar and cinnamon in large bowl. Stir in pumpkin, eggs, water and vanilla extract just until moistened. Stir in half of baking bars and *half* of pecans. Spread into greased 13 x 9-inch baking pan.

BAKE in preheated 350°F. oven for 20 minutes. Sprinkle with *remaining* baking bars and remaining pecans. Bake for 10 to 15 minutes more or until wooden pick inserted in center comes out clean. Cool completely in pan on wire rack. Makes 16 servings.

pumpkin apple gingerbread

3½ cups all-purpose flour
1 tablespoon baking powder
2½ teaspoons ground ginger
½ teaspoon baking soda
½ teaspoon salt
½ teaspoon pumpkin pie spice
1 cup (2 sticks) butter or margarine, softened
1 cup granulated sugar
½ cup packed brown sugar

4 eggs
1¾ cups (15-ounce can) LIBBY'S® Solid Pack Pumpkin
1 large baking apple (such as Granny Smith), peeled and shredded (about 1 cup)
½ cup molasses
Powdered sugar
Hard Sauce (recipe follows)

COMBINE flour, baking powder, ginger, baking soda, salt and pumpkin pie spice in medium bowl.

BEAT butter, granulated sugar and brown sugar in large mixer bowl until light and fluffy. Add eggs, two at a time, beating well after each addition. Beat in pumpkin, apple and molasses. Gradually beat in flour mixture.

SPOON batter into well-greased and floured 12-cup fluted tube pan.* Bake in preheated 350°F. oven for 1 hour or until wooden pick inserted in cake comes out clean. Cool in pan on wire rack for 15 minutes; remove from pan. Dust with powdered sugar. Serve warm with Hard Sauce. Makes 12 servings.

*Note: Recipe also may be made in two 8- or 9-inch round cake pans or one 13 x 9-inch baking pan. Bake in preheated 350°F. oven for 40 to 45 minutes or until wooden pick inserted in cake comes out clean.

For Hard Sauce:
BEAT 1 cup (2 sticks) softened butter and 2 teaspoons vanilla extract in small mixer bowl until smooth. Gradually beat in 4 cups sifted powdered sugar until fluffy.

pumpkin orange cake roll

CAKE ROLL
- 1 package (16 ounces) angel food cake mix
- 2½ teaspoons grated orange peel, *divided*
- ½ cup powdered sugar

FILLING
- 1½ cups LIBBY'S® Solid Pack Pumpkin
- ½ cup granulated sugar
- 1 teaspoon ground cinnamon
- 1 teaspoon vanilla extract
- Powdered sugar
- 2 tablespoons currant or grape jelly (optional)

For Cake Roll:

PREPARE cake mix according to package directions, adding *1½ teaspoons* orange peel at end of mixing time. Spread batter evenly into foil-lined 15 x 10-inch jelly-roll pan. (Foil should extend 1 inch above edge of pan.)

BAKE at oven temperature suggested in package directions for 30 minutes or until top of cake springs back when touched. While cake is baking, sprinkle towel with powdered sugar. Immediately turn cake out onto towel. Carefully peel off foil. Roll up cake and towel together, starting with a narrow end. Cool on wire rack.

For Filling:

COMBINE pumpkin, granulated sugar, cinnamon, vanilla extract and *remaining* orange peel in medium bowl.

To Assemble:

CAREFULLY unroll cake and spread with Filling. Reroll cake. Sprinkle with powdered sugar. Stir jelly well; spoon into small, heavy-duty plastic bag. Cut a small hole in corner of bag; squeeze to drizzle jelly over cake roll. Makes 10 servings. Per serving: 0.5 grams fat and 250 calories.

pumpkin orange poppy seed cake

1 package (18¼ ounces) yellow cake mix

1¼ cups LIBBY'S® Solid Pack Pumpkin

⅔ cup orange juice

3 eggs

¼ cup poppy seeds

Orange Glaze (recipe follows)

Low-fat frozen yogurt (optional)

COMBINE cake mix, pumpkin, orange juice and eggs in large mixer bowl; beat on low speed for 30 seconds. Beat on medium speed for 2 minutes. Add poppy seeds; mix until blended. Spread batter into greased and floured 12-cup fluted tube pan.

BAKE in preheated 350°F. oven for 35 to 40 minutes or until wooden pick inserted in cake comes out clean. Cool in pan on wire rack for 10 minutes. Invert onto wire rack to cool completely. Frost top of cake with Orange Glaze. Serve with frozen yogurt, if desired. Makes 24 servings. Per serving: 4 grams fat and 140 calories.

For Orange Glaze:
COMBINE 1½ cups sifted powdered sugar and 2 to 3 tablespoons orange juice in small bowl until smooth.

Add Pumpkin, Cut the Fat

Add flavor and minimize the fat in packaged muffin and cake mixes! Simply replace the oil called for in the package directions with an equal amount of pumpkin. The result is a moist and delicious cake or muffin with less fat. Adding pumpkin to mixes in place of the fat also results in a wonderful moist texture. To taste for yourself, try the Pumpkin Orange Poppy Seed Cake. Because the pumpkin keeps it moist, this cake tastes every bit as good the second day!

quick pumpkin cupcakes

1 package (16 ounces) pound cake mix
1 cup LIBBY'S® Solid Pack Pumpkin
2 eggs
⅓ cup water

2 teaspoons pumpkin pie spice
1 teaspoon baking soda
1 container (16 ounces) prepared vanilla frosting

BEAT cake mix, pumpkin, eggs, water, pumpkin pie spice and baking soda in large mixer bowl on medium speed for 3 minutes. Pour batter into 12 to 14 paper-lined muffin cups.

BAKE in preheated 325°F. oven for 25 to 30 minutes or until golden brown. Cool in pan on wire rack for 10 minutes. Remove to wire rack to cool completely. Spread cupcakes with frosting. Top with walnut halves. Makes 12 to 14 cupcakes.

golden pound cake

3 cups cake flour or 2⅔ cups all-purpose flour
1½ teaspoons baking powder
¼ teaspoon salt
¼ teaspoon ground mace or ground nutmeg
1½ cups granulated sugar
1 cup (2 sticks) butter or margarine, softened
1 teaspoon vanilla extract
3 eggs
½ cup NESTLÉ® CARNATION® Evaporated Milk
¾ cup walnuts or pecans
Cinnamon Custard Sauce (optional recipe follows)

For Cake:
COMBINE flour, baking powder, salt and mace in medium bowl. Beat sugar, butter and vanilla extract in large mixer bowl until light and fluffy. Add eggs, one at a time, beating well after each addition.

ADD flour mixture alternately with evaporated milk, beating well after each addition. Pour batter into greased 9 × 5-inch loaf pan; sprinkle with nuts.

BAKE in preheated 350°F. oven for 60 to 70 minutes or until wooden pick inserted near center comes out clean. Cool in pan on wire rack for 10 minutes. Remove to wire rack to cool completely. Serve with Cinnamon Custard Sauce, if desired. Makes 12 servings.

For Cinnamon Custard Sauce:
COMBINE ⅓ cup granulated sugar, 2 teaspoons cornstarch and ½ teaspoon ground cinnamon in medium saucepan; gradually stir in 1 cup NESTLÉ® CARNATION® evaporated milk, ⅓ cup water and 1 egg yolk, lightly beaten. Bring to a boil over medium heat, stirring constantly, until mixture is slightly thickened. Remove from heat; stir in 1 teaspoon vanilla extract. Serve sauce over slices of cake.

glazed chocolate sweet cakes

CAKES

- 2 cups (12 ounce package) NESTLÉ® TOLL HOUSE® Semi-Sweet Chocolate Morsels, *divided*
- 1 ½ cups all-purpose flour
- 1 teaspoon baking soda
- 1 teaspoon salt
- ½ cup granulated sugar
- ⅓ cup vegetable oil
- 1 egg
- 1 teaspoon vanilla extract
- 1 cup water

GLAZE

- ⅔ cup heavy whipping cream
- 2 tablespoons butter or margarine
- 2 tablespoons light corn syrup
- Sweetened whipped cream (optional)
- Orange peel curls (optional)

For Cakes:

MICROWAVE *1 cup* morsels in small, microwave-safe bowl on HIGH (100%) power for 1 minute; stir. Microwave at additional 10- to 20-second intervals, stirring until smooth. Cool to room temperature. Combine flour, baking soda and salt in small bowl.

BEAT sugar, oil, egg and vanilla extract in large mixer bowl until blended. Beat in melted chocolate. Gradually beat in flour mixture alternately with water. Spoon into 12 greased muffin cups.

BAKE in preheated 350°F. oven for 18 to 22 minutes or until wooden pick inserted in center comes out clean. Let stand for 20 minutes. Remove from pan; turn upside down on wire rack to cool completely. Trim edges with scissors, if necessary.

For Glaze:

HEAT *remaining* morsels, cream, butter and corn syrup in medium, *heavy-duty* saucepan over medium heat until mixture comes to a boil, stirring constantly. Remove from heat; stir until smooth. Cool to room temperature. Spread over sides and flat tops of cakes or dip cakes into glaze. Garnish with whipped cream and orange peel curls just before serving. Makes 12 minicakes.

marbled chocolate sour cream cake

1 cup (6 ounces) NESTLÉ® TOLL HOUSE® Semi-Sweet
  Chocolate Morsels
1 package (18½ ounces) yellow cake mix
4 eggs
¾ cup sour cream
½ cup vegetable oil
¼ cup water
¼ cup granulated sugar
  Sifted powdered sugar

MICROWAVE morsels in medium, microwave-safe bowl on HIGH
(100%) power for 1 minute; stir. Microwave at additional 10- to
20-second intervals, stirring until smooth.

COMBINE cake mix, eggs, sour cream, oil, water and granulated
sugar in large mixer bowl. Beat on low speed until moistened. Beat
on high speed for 2 minutes.

STIR 2 cups batter into melted chocolate. Alternately spoon
batters into greased 10-cup bundt or round tube pan.

BAKE in preheated 375°F. oven for 35 to 45 minutes or until
wooden pick inserted in center comes out clean. Cool in pan on
wire rack for 20 minutes. Invert onto wire rack to cool completely.
Sprinkle with powdered sugar before serving. Makes 24 servings.

white chip spice cake

1 package (18¼ ounces) spice cake mix
1 cup LIBBY'S® Solid Pack Pumpkin
3 eggs
⅔ cup NESTLÉ® CARNATION® Evaporated Milk, *divided*
⅓ cup vegetable oil
2 cups (12-ounce package) NESTLÉ® TOLL HOUSE® Premier White Morsels, *divided*
½ teaspoon ground cinnamon

BEAT cake mix, pumpkin, eggs, *⅓ cup* evaporated milk and vegetable oil in large mixer bowl on low speed until moistened. Beat on medium speed for 2 minutes; stir in *1 cup* morsels. Pour into greased and floured 12-cup fluted tube pan.

BAKE in preheated 350°F. oven for 40 to 45 minutes or until wooden pick inserted in cake comes out clean. Cool in pan on wire rack for 25 minutes. Invert onto wire rack to cool completely.

HEAT *remaining* evaporated milk in small, *heavy-duty* saucepan over medium heat just to a boil; remove from heat. Add *remaining* morsels, stirring until smooth and melted. Stir in cinnamon. Drizzle some of the mixture over cake; serve cake with remaining mixture. Makes 18 servings.

White Chip Spice Cake (see recipe above) and
Pumpkin Cheesecake (see recipe, page 197)

cinnamon chocolate cake

CHOCOLATE CAKE

- 1 cup (6 ounces) NESTLÉ® TOLL HOUSE® Semi-Sweet Chocolate Morsels
- 1¼ cups granulated sugar
- ¾ cup (1½ sticks) butter or margarine, softened
- 1 teaspoon vanilla extract
- 3 eggs
- 2 cups all-purpose flour
- 1 tablespoon ground cinnamon
- 1 teaspoon baking soda
- ½ teaspoon salt
- 1 cup milk
- 1 to 2 tablespoons ORTEGA® Diced Jalapeños (optional)

CHOCOLATE FROSTING

- 3 to 3¼ cups sifted powdered sugar
- ½ cup milk
- ¼ cup (½ stick) butter or margarine, softened
- 2 packets (1 ounce *each*) NESTLÉ® TOLL HOUSE® CHOCO BAKE® Unsweetened Chocolate Flavor
- 2 teaspoons vanilla extract
- ¼ teaspoon salt
- 1¼ cups sliced almonds, toasted

For Chocolate Cake:

MICROWAVE morsels in medium, microwave-safe bowl on HIGH (100%) power for 1 minute; stir. Microwave at additional 10- to 20-second intervals, stirring until smooth. Beat sugar, butter and vanilla extract in large mixer bowl. Add eggs; beat for 1 minute. Beat in melted chocolate. Combine flour, cinnamon, baking soda and salt in medium bowl; beat into chocolate mixture alternately with milk. Stir in jalapeños. Pour into 2 well-greased 9-inch round cake pans.

BAKE in preheated 350°F. oven for 30 to 35 minutes or until wooden pick inserted in center comes out clean. Cool in pans on wire racks for 20 minutes. Invert onto wire racks to cool completely.

For Chocolate Frosting:

BEAT powdered sugar, milk, butter, chocolate flavor, vanilla extract and salt in small mixer bowl until mixture is smooth and creamy. Frost cake. Decorate sides with nuts. Makes 12 servings.

vermont spice cake

CAKE
1½ cups granulated sugar
¾ cup (1½ sticks) butter, softened
3 eggs
1½ cups LIBBY'S® Solid Pack Pumpkin
1½ teaspoons vanilla extract
½ cup NESTLÉ® CARNATION® Evaporated Milk
¼ cup water
3 cups all-purpose flour
3½ teaspoons baking powder
1½ teaspoons ground cinnamon
1 teaspoon baking soda
¾ teaspoon ground nutmeg
½ teaspoon salt
¼ teaspoon ground cloves
¼ teaspoon ground ginger
   Chopped nuts and/or nut halves (optional)

MAPLE FROSTING
1 package (8 ounces) *and* 1 package (3 ounces) cream cheese, softened
⅓ cup butter, softened
3½ cups sifted powdered sugar
2 to 3 teaspoons maple flavoring

For Cake:
BEAT sugar and butter in large mixer bowl until creamy. Add eggs; beat for 2 minutes. Add pumpkin and vanilla extract; mix well. Beat in evaporated milk and water.

COMBINE flour, baking powder, cinnamon, baking soda, nutmeg, salt, cloves and ginger in a large bowl. Beat into pumpkin mixture.

SPREAD pumpkin mixture evenly into 2 greased and floured 9-inch round cake pans. Bake in preheated 325°F. oven for 35 to 40 minutes or until wooden pick inserted in center comes out clean. Cool in pans on wire racks for 15 minutes. Invert onto wire racks to cool completely.

For Maple Frosting:
BEAT cream cheese and butter in large mixer bowl; gradually beat in powdered sugar. Beat in maple flavoring until fluffy.

To Assemble:
CUT cakes in half horizontally with long serrated knife. Frost between layers and on top of cake, leaving sides unfrosted. Top with nuts. Store in refrigerator. Makes 12 servings.

distinctive desserts

when friends and family

gather for a special meal, serve a dessert

worth remembering. Pumpkin Pear Strudel,

Toffee Cheesecake or Summer Berry

Brownie Torte are a few exquisite creations

that will leave a lasting impression. You

can make all of these recipes before your

guests arrive, so you, too, can relax and

join in the fun and conversation.

Pumpkin Apple Dessert Pizza (see recipe, page 186)

pumpkin apple dessert pizza

1 roll (18 ounces) refrigerated NESTLÉ® TOLL HOUSE® Sugar
Cookie Dough

1 cup LIBBY'S® Solid Pack Pumpkin

1 package (3 ounces) cream cheese, softened

3 tablespoons granulated sugar, *divided*

½ teaspoon ground cinnamon

1 medium green apple, peeled and thinly sliced (about 1 cup)
Dash ground cinnamon

⅓ cup chopped walnuts

1 to 2 tablespoons caramel-flavored ice-cream
topping

FREEZE cookie dough for 30 minutes; slice into ¼-inch-thick
pieces (about 32). Place slices, edges touching, on greased 12-inch
pizza pan.* Bake in preheated 350°F. oven for 12 to 15 minutes
or until golden brown. Remove from oven; prick with fork. Cool
on wire rack.

BEAT pumpkin, cream cheese, *2 tablespoons* sugar and ½ teaspoon
cinnamon in small mixer bowl until smooth. Spread over pizza
crust to within ¾ inch of edge. Mix apple slices with *remaining*
sugar and dash cinnamon in small bowl; place on pizza. Sprinkle
with walnuts.

BAKE at 350°F. for 8 minutes more. Place on wire rack. Drizzle
with caramel topping. Cool slightly. Cut into wedges; serve warm.
Makes 12 servings.

*Note: Recipe also may be made in 13 x 9-inch baking pan. Bake
crust in preheated 350°F. oven for 15 to 17 minutes or until golden
brown. Add apple topping and bake for 10 minutes more.

Pictured on pages 184 and 185.

pumpkin oatmeal spice tortes

1¾ cups (15-ounce can) LIBBY'S® Solid Pack Pumpkin
¾ cup packed brown sugar
1½ teaspoons ground cinnamon
1 package (18¼ ounces) spice cake mix
2 eggs
½ cup (1 stick) butter or margarine, softened
Oatmeal Topping (recipe follows)

COMBINE pumpkin, brown sugar and cinnamon in medium bowl.

COMBINE cake mix, eggs and butter in large mixer bowl; beat on low speed until blended (batter will be stiff). Spread into 2 greased 9-inch round cake pans.

BAKE in preheated 350°F. oven for 15 minutes; remove from oven. Spread with pumpkin mixture; sprinkle with Oatmeal Topping. Return to oven; bake for 15 minutes more. Cool in pans on wire racks. Makes 12 servings.

For Oatmeal Topping:
COMBINE 1 cup quick or old-fashioned oats, ¾ cup packed brown sugar, ½ cup chopped walnuts, ¼ cup melted butter or margarine and 1 teaspoon ground cinnamon.

Measuring Oats

Measure quick or old-fashioned oats as you do flour by spooning the oats into a dry measuring cup, then leveling with a straight-edged spatula. If you use the scoop-and-shake method, you will use more oats than necessary, which causes a dry topping, cookie or cake.

pumpkin pear strudel

  2 small pears, peeled and diced (about 2 cups)
  1 cup LIBBY'S® Solid Pack Pumpkin
  ¾ cup packed brown sugar
  ¾ cup chopped walnuts
  1 teaspoon ground cinnamon
  ⅛ teaspoon ground cloves
  ⅛ teaspoon ground ginger
  1 package (17¼ ounces) frozen puff pastry, thawed according to package directions (2 sheets)
  1 egg, lightly beaten
    Cinnamon Sugar (recipe follows)

MIX pears, pumpkin, brown sugar, walnuts, cinnamon, cloves and ginger in medium bowl. Spoon *half* of the pear mixture down the center ⅓ of 1 pastry sheet. Make downward slanting cuts in outer edges of pastry about ¾ inch apart, cutting from outside edges to within about 1 inch of pear mixture. Starting at top, fold side pastry strips alternately over filling, forming chevron design (see photo, *below*). Seal top and bottom ends of strudel. Place on rimmed baking sheet. Repeat with *remaining* pear mixture and *remaining* pastry sheet. Brush both strudels with egg; sprinkle with Cinnamon Sugar.

BAKE in preheated 375°F. oven for 25 to 30 minutes or until golden brown and puffy. Cool slightly on baking sheets on wire racks. Serve warm or at room temperature. Makes 10 servings.

For Cinnamon Sugar:
COMBINE ¼ cup granulated sugar and ¾ teaspoon ground cinnamon in a small bowl.

To shape each strudel, starting at the top of the pastry sheet (pastry strips should be slanting down), fold the side pastry strips alternately over the filling to form a chevron design. Seal the top and bottom ends of the strudel.

distinctive desserts

pumpkin pecan bread pudding

½ loaf Italian or French bread, cut into ¾-inch cubes (about 5 cups)

1¾ cups (15-ounce can) LIBBY'S® Solid Pack Pumpkin, *divided*

1½ cups (12 fluid-ounce can) NESTLÉ® CARNATION® Evaporated Milk

3 eggs

½ cup packed brown sugar

½ cup coarsely chopped pecans

1 teaspoon vanilla extract

¾ teaspoon ground cinnamon

¼ teaspoon ground nutmeg

Pumpkin Caramel Sauce (recipe follows)

PLACE bread in greased 8-inch square baking pan. Combine *1 cup* pumpkin, evaporated milk, eggs, brown sugar, pecans, vanilla extract, cinnamon and nutmeg in medium bowl. Pour over bread; press bread into egg mixture. Place square pan into 13 x 9-inch baking pan; fill outer pan with hot water to 1-inch depth. Bake in preheated 350°F. oven for 45 to 50 minutes or until set. Serve with Pumpkin Caramel Sauce. Makes 6 servings.

For Pumpkin Caramel Sauce:

COMBINE ½ cup caramel- or butterscotch-flavored ice-cream topping, *remaining* pumpkin and ¼ teaspoon ground cinnamon in medium saucepan. Warm over low heat, stirring frequently. *Do not allow mixture to boil.*

mocha bread pudding
with caramel sauce

BREAD PUDDING

 9 cups (about ¾ of a 1-pound loaf) French bread, cut into
    1-inch cubes
 1 cup granulated sugar
 ¼ cup NESTLÉ® TOLL HOUSE® Baking Cocoa
 1 tablespoon TASTER'S CHOICE® Original Blend Freeze Dried
    Coffee
 4 eggs
 3 cups (*two* 12 fluid-ounce cans) NESTLÉ® CARNATION®
    Evaporated Skimmed Milk or Evaporated Lowfat Milk,
    divided
 2 teaspoons vanilla extract

CARAMEL SAUCE

 ⅔ cup packed brown sugar
 ¼ cup (½ stick) butter or margarine
 1 tablespoon light corn syrup

For Bread Pudding:
PLACE bread cubes in greased 2-quart baking dish. Combine sugar, cocoa and coffee granules in small bowl.

BEAT eggs, *2⅔ cups* evaporated milk and vanilla extract in medium bowl until well blended; stir in sugar mixture. Pour over bread, pressing bread into milk mixture.

BAKE in preheated 350°F. oven for 50 to 55 minutes or until set.

For Caramel Sauce:
COMBINE brown sugar, butter and corn syrup in small saucepan. Cook over medium-low heat, stirring constantly, for 2 to 3 minutes or until sugar is dissolved. Slowly stir in *remaining* evaporated milk. Bring to a boil, stirring constantly; cook for 1 minute. Remove from heat. Serve with warm bread pudding. Makes 12 servings.

summer berry brownie torte

¾ cup granulated sugar

6 tablespoons butter or margarine

1 tablespoon water

1½ cups (9 ounces) NESTLÉ® TOLL HOUSE® Semi-Sweet Chocolate Morsels, *divided*

½ teaspoon vanilla extract

2 eggs

⅔ cup all-purpose flour

¼ teaspoon baking soda

¼ teaspoon salt

Filling (recipe follows)

2 cups sliced strawberries or blueberries

COMBINE sugar, butter and water in small, *heavy-duty* saucepan. Bring to a boil, stirring constantly; remove from heat. Add ¾ *cup* morsels; stir until smooth. Stir in vanilla extract. Add eggs, one at a time, stirring well after each addition. Add flour, baking soda and salt; stir until well blended. Stir in *remaining* morsels. Pour into waxed paper-lined and greased 9-inch round cake pan.

BAKE in preheated 350°F. oven for 20 to 25 minutes or until wooden pick inserted in center comes out slightly sticky. Cool in pan on wire rack for 15 minutes. Invert onto wire rack; remove waxed paper. Turn right side up; cool completely. Spread Filling over brownie; top with berries. Chill until serving time. Makes 8 to 10 servings.

For Filling:
BEAT ½ cup heavy whipping cream and ¼ cup granulated sugar in small mixer bowl until stiff peaks form.

tuxedo cheesecake

CRUST

1¾ cups (about 18) crushed creme-filled chocolate cookies

2 tablespoons butter or margarine, melted

FILLING

1 cup (6 ounces) NESTLÉ® TOLL HOUSE® Premier White Morsels

3 packages (8 ounces *each*) cream cheese, softened

¾ cup granulated sugar

2 teaspoon vanilla extract

3 eggs

1 bar (2 ounces) NESTLÉ® TOLL HOUSE® Semi-Sweet or Premier White Baking Bars, made into curls or grated

For Crust:

TOSS cookie crumbs and butter together in medium bowl. Press onto bottom of ungreased 9-inch springform pan. Bake in preheated 350°F. oven for 10 minutes.

For Filling:

MICROWAVE morsels in small, microwave-safe bowl on MEDIUM-HIGH (70%) power for 1 minute; stir. Microwave at additional 10- to 20-second intervals, stirring until smooth; cool to room temperature.

BEAT cream cheese, sugar and vanilla extract in large mixer bowl until smooth. Beat in eggs. Gradually beat in melted white morsels. Spread over chocolate crust.

BAKE in 350°F. oven for 40 to 50 minutes or until edges are set but center still moves slightly. Cool in pan on wire rack; chill until firm. Remove side of springform pan. Garnish with chocolate curls* before serving. Makes 14 to 16 servings.

*Note: To make chocolate curls, carefully draw a vegetable peeler across a bar of NESTLÉ® TOLL HOUSE® Semi-Sweet Chocolate. Vary the width of your curls by using different sides of the chocolate bar.

pumpkin orange cheesecake

Lower Fat

CRUST
- ¾ cup graham cracker crumbs
- 2 tablespoons margarine or butter, melted

FILLING
- 2 packages (8 ounces *each*) light cream cheese (Neufchâtel), softened
- ¾ cup packed brown sugar
- ½ cup nonfat ricotta cheese
- 1½ cups LIBBY'S® Solid Pack Pumpkin
- 3 tablespoons orange juice
- 2 tablespoons NESTLÉ® CARNATION® Evaporated Skimmed Milk
- 2 teaspoons vanilla extract
- 1½ teaspoons pumpkin pie spice
- 1 teaspoon grated orange peel
- ¾ cup frozen egg substitute, thawed

Orange Topping (recipe follows)

For Crust:
COMBINE graham cracker crumbs and margarine in small bowl. Press onto bottom of 9-inch springform pan.

For Filling:
BEAT cream cheese, brown sugar and ricotta cheese in large mixer bowl until fluffy. Add pumpkin, orange juice, evaporated skimmed milk, vanilla extract, pumpkin pie spice and orange peel; beat until well blended. Add egg substitute and beat just until blended. Pour into prepared crust.

BAKE in preheated 350°F. oven for 60 to 65 minutes or until edge is set but center still moves slightly. Cool in pan on wire rack; spread with Orange Topping. Chill several hours or overnight; remove side of pan. Makes 12 servings. Per serving: 5 grams fat and 200 calories.

For Orange Topping:
COMBINE ½ cup light sour cream, 1 tablespoon granulated sugar and 1 teaspoon orange juice.

pumpkin cheesecake

CRUST

1½ cups graham cracker crumbs

⅓ cup butter or margarine, melted

¼ cup granulated sugar

CHEESECAKE

3 packages (8 ounces *each*) cream cheese, softened

1 cup granulated sugar

¼ cup packed brown sugar

1¾ cups (15-ounce can) LIBBY'S® Solid Pack Pumpkin

2 eggs

⅔ cup NESTLÉ® CARNATION® Evaporated Milk

2 tablespoons cornstarch

1¼ teaspoons ground cinnamon

½ teaspoon ground nutmeg

TOPPING

2 cups (16-ounce carton) sour cream, at room temperature

¼ to ⅓ cup granulated sugar

1 teaspoon vanilla extract

Whole strawberries, sliced and fanned (optional)

For Crust:
COMBINE graham cracker crumbs, butter and granulated sugar in medium bowl. Press onto bottom and 1 inch up side of 9-inch springform pan. Bake in preheated 350°F. oven for 6 to 8 minutes. Do not allow to brown. Cool on wire rack.

For Cheesecake:
BEAT cream cheese, granulated sugar and brown sugar in large mixer bowl until fluffy. Beat in pumpkin, eggs and evaporated milk. Add cornstarch, cinnamon and nutmeg; beat well. Pour into crust.

BAKE at 350°F. for 55 to 60 minutes or until edge is set but center still moves slightly.

For Topping:
COMBINE sour cream, granulated sugar and vanilla extract in small bowl. Spread over surface of warm cheesecake. Bake at 350°F. for 8 minutes more. Cool in pan on wire rack. Chill for several hours or overnight; remove side of pan. Garnish with strawberries. Makes 16 servings.

Pictured on page 178.

toffee cheesecake

CRUST
1¾ cups finely crushed toffee
shortbread cookies
(about 14 to 16 cookies)
4 teaspoons butter or
margarine, melted

CHEESECAKE
3 packages (8 ounces *each*)
cream cheese, softened
1¼ cups packed brown sugar
1¾ cups (15-ounce can)
LIBBY'S® Solid Pack
Pumpkin
2 eggs
⅔ cup NESTLÉ®
CARNATION®
Evaporated Milk

2 tablespoons cornstarch
½ teaspoon ground
cinnamon
⅔ cup chopped or crushed
toffee candies
(about 24 candies),
divided

TOPPING
2 cups (16-ounce carton)
sour cream, at room
temperature
¼ cup granulated sugar
½ teaspoon vanilla extract
Caramel-flavored
ice-cream topping
(optional)

For Crust:
COMBINE crushed cookies and butter in small bowl. Press onto
bottom and 1 inch up side of 9-inch springform pan. Bake in
preheated 350°F. oven for 6 to 8 minutes. Do not allow to brown.
Cool on wire rack.

For Cheesecake:
BEAT cream cheese and brown sugar in large mixer bowl on
medium speed until creamy. Beat in pumpkin, eggs, evaporated
milk, cornstarch and cinnamon. Stir in ⅓ *cup* toffee pieces. Pour
into prepared crust.

BAKE at 350°F. for 60 to 65 minutes or until edge is set but center
still moves slightly.

For Topping:
COMBINE sour cream, granulated sugar, vanilla extract and
remaining toffee pieces in small bowl. Spread over surface of warm
cheesecake. Bake at 350°F. for 8 minutes more. Cool in pan
on wire rack. Chill several hours or overnight; remove side of
pan. Before serving, drizzle with caramel topping, if desired.
Makes 16 servings.

maple cheesecake

Lower Fat

¾ cup graham cracker
crumbs

2 tablespoons margarine or
butter, melted

1¾ cups (15-ounce can)
LIBBY'S® Solid Pack
Pumpkin

2 packages (8 ounces *each*)
light cream cheese
(Neufchâtel)

1 cup packed brown sugar

½ cup part-skim-milk ricotta
cheese

2 tablespoons all-purpose
flour

1½ teaspoons pumpkin pie
spice

1½ teaspoons maple
flavoring

½ cup NESTLÉ®
CARNATION®
Evaporated Skimmed
Milk or Evaporated
Lowfat Milk

½ cup egg substitute
Maple Topping (recipe
follows)
Chopped pecans
(optional)

COMBINE crumbs and margarine in small bowl. Press onto
bottom of 9-inch springform pan.

BEAT pumpkin, cream cheese, brown sugar, ricotta cheese, flour,
pumpkin pie spice and maple flavoring in large mixer bowl on high
speed for 1 minute. Beat in evaporated skimmed milk and egg
substitute just until blended. Pour over crust.

BAKE in preheated 350°F. oven for 65 to 85 minutes or until knife
inserted halfway between center and outer edge comes out clean.
Remove from oven; cool in pan on wire rack for 10 minutes.
Spread with Maple Topping; chill. To serve, remove side of pan and
sprinkle with pecans. Makes 16 servings. Per serving: 10 grams fat
and 210 calories.

For Maple Topping:
COMBINE ½ cup nonfat sour cream, 1 tablespoon granulated
sugar and ¼ teaspoon maple flavoring in small bowl.

mini cream cheese flans

   1 cup granulated sugar

  ½ cup water

1½ cups (12 fluid-ounce can) NESTLÉ® CARNATION®
      Evaporated Milk

1¼ cups (14-ounce can) NESTLÉ® CARNATION® Sweetened
      Condensed Milk

   1 package (8 ounces) cream cheese, softened

  ¼ cup (½ stick) butter, softened

   5 eggs

   1 teaspoon vanilla extract

FILL two 13 x 9-inch baking pans with hot water to 1-inch depth. Place twelve 6-ounce custard cups in prepared pans.

COMBINE sugar and water in small saucepan. Cook, stirring constantly, over low heat for 2 minutes or until sugar is dissolved. Bring to a boil. Boil, without stirring, for 10 to 15 minutes or until golden brown. Quickly pour evenly into custard cups.

COMBINE evaporated milk, sweetened condensed milk, cream cheese, butter, eggs and vanilla extract in blender container; cover. Blend until smooth. Pour into prepared cups.

BAKE in preheated 350°F. oven for 35 to 45 minutes or until knife inserted near center comes out clean. Cool in pans on wire racks for 20 minutes. Remove custard cups from baking pans; chill for several hours or overnight. Run knife around rims; shake gently to loosen. Invert onto serving dishes. Makes 12 servings.

cream cheese flan

¾ cup granulated sugar

1½ cups (12 fluid-ounce can) NESTLÉ® CARNATION® Evaporated Milk

1¼ cups (14-ounce can) NESTLÉ® CARNATION® Sweetened Condensed Milk

1 package (8 ounces) cream cheese, softened, cut into chunks

5 eggs

PLACE sugar in small, *heavy-duty* saucepan. Cook over medium-high heat, stirring constantly, for 3 to 4 minutes or until sugar is dissolved and golden. Quickly pour into eight 10-ounce custard cups;* tip cups to coat bottoms and sides with sugar syrup.

PLACE evaporated milk, sweetened condensed milk and cream cheese in food processor or blender container; cover. Process until smooth. Add eggs; process until well mixed. Pour mixture into prepared cups. Place cups in 2 large baking pans; fill pans with hot water to 1-inch depth.

BAKE in preheated 350°F. oven for 30 to 40 minutes or until knife inserted in centers comes out clean. Remove to wire racks to cool for 30 minutes; chill for several hours or overnight. To serve, run small spatula around edges of cups; gently shake flans to loosen. Invert onto serving dishes to serve. Makes 8 servings.

*Note: To make one large flan, use one 2-quart casserole dish instead of custard cups. Coat with melted sugar syrup and pour milk mixture into dish as above. Place dish in large baking pan; fill pan halfway with hot water. Bake in preheated 350°F. oven for 60 to 70 minutes or until knife inserted in center comes out clean. Cool. Chill; invert as above onto a serving platter. Slice into wedges. Makes 8 servings.

pumpkin caramel flan

¾ cup granulated sugar

4 eggs

1 cup LIBBY'S® Solid Pack Pumpkin

⅓ cup honey

1 to 1½ teaspoons pumpkin pie spice

1 teaspoon vanilla extract

½ teaspoon salt

1½ cups (12 fluid-ounce can) NESTLÉ® CARNATION® Evaporated Milk

Nasturtium blossoms (optional)

PLACE 8-inch square baking dish into 13 x 9-inch baking dish; fill outer dish with hot water to ¾-inch depth.

HEAT sugar in heavy skillet over medium heat, stirring constantly, until melted and golden brown; pour into square dish. Remove square dish from water; working quickly, swirl melted sugar around bottom and sides of dish to coat. Return dish to water.

COMBINE eggs, pumpkin, honey, pumpkin pie spice, vanilla extract and salt in medium bowl. Add evaporated milk; mix well. Pour into prepared square baking dish.

BAKE in preheated 350°F. oven for 40 to 45 minutes or until knife inserted near center comes out clean. Remove square baking dish from water. Cool in baking dish on wire rack. Cover and chill for 4 hours or overnight. To serve, run small spatula around edge of dish. Invert serving plate over baking dish. Invert baking dish; shake gently to release. Cut flan diagonally into quarters; cut each quarter in half to form triangles. Spoon some of the caramel syrup from baking dish over each serving. Garnish with edible nasturtium blossoms, if desired (see tip on edible flowers, *page 150*). Makes 8 servings.

For Lower-Fat Flan:
USE 2 eggs and 2 egg whites in place of the 4 eggs and NESTLÉ® CARNATION® Evaporated Skimmed Milk in place of the evaporated milk. Prepare and bake as above. Makes 8 servings. Per serving: 1.5 grams fat and 190 calories.

best of breads

a loaf of bread baking,

with its soul-soothing aroma, draws

everyone to the kitchen in anticipation.

Treat loved ones to a batch of gooey

cinnamon rolls or a loaf of pumpkin bread

made special with Libby's® Pumpkin. This

baker's assortment of recipes offers

breads, rolls, muffins, biscuits and other

baked goods, just right for mealtime or

anytime snacking.

*Pumpkin Swirl Breakfast Rolls (see recipe, page 210) and
Pumpkin Honey Wheat Bread (see recipe, page 208)*

pumpkin honey wheat bread

2¼ cups all-purpose flour
¾ cup wheat germ
2½ teaspoons baking powder
1½ teaspoons ground cinnamon
1 teaspoon salt
½ teaspoon baking soda
1¼ cups LIBBY'S® Solid Pack Pumpkin
¾ cup honey
2 eggs
¼ cup vegetable oil
¼ cup milk
¼ cup pine nuts or sunflower seeds

COMBINE flour, wheat germ, baking powder, cinnamon, salt and baking soda in large bowl. Combine pumpkin, honey, eggs, vegetable oil and milk in medium bowl; add to flour mixture. Stir just until blended.

SPREAD batter into greased 9 x 5-inch loaf pan. Sprinkle with pine nuts; gently pat into batter. Bake in preheated 350°F. oven for 55 to 60 minutes or until wooden pick inserted in center comes out clean. Cool in pan on wire rack for 10 minutes; remove to wire rack to cool completely. Makes 1 loaf.

Pictured on pages 206 and 207.

pumpkin nut mini loaves

3¼ cups all-purpose flour
¾ cup quick or old-fashioned oats
2 teaspoons baking soda
1½ teaspoons pumpkin pie spice
½ teaspoon baking powder
½ teaspoon salt
1¾ cups (15-ounce can) LIBBY'S® Solid Pack Pumpkin
1½ cups granulated sugar
1½ cups packed brown sugar
3 eggs
½ cup water
½ cup vegetable oil
½ cup NESTLÉ® CARNATION® Evaporated Milk
1 cup chopped walnuts

COMBINE flour, oats, baking soda, pumpkin pie spice, baking powder and salt in large bowl. Beat pumpkin, granulated sugar, brown sugar, eggs, water, vegetable oil and evaporated milk in large mixer bowl on medium speed until combined. Gradually beat flour mixture into pumpkin mixture on low speed; stir in walnuts. Spread into 6 greased 5⅝ x 3¼-inch mini loaf pans.*

BAKE in preheated 350°F. oven for 40 to 45 minutes or until wooden pick inserted in center comes out clean. Cool in pans on wire racks for 10 minutes. Remove to racks to cool completely. Makes 6 loaves.

*Note: To make regular-size loaves, prepare recipe and spread batter into 2 greased 9 x 5-inch loaf pans. Bake in preheated 350°F. oven for 65 to 70 minutes or until wooden pick inserted in center comes out clean. Cool as above. Makes 2 loaves.

pumpkin swirl breakfast rolls

½ cup packed brown sugar
¾ teaspoon ground cinnamon
⅛ teaspoon ground cloves
⅓ cup butter or margarine
1 cup LIBBY'S® Solid Pack Pumpkin
¾ cup chopped walnuts or pecans
⅓ cup raisins
1 pound frozen bread dough, thawed
Glaze (recipe follows)

COMBINE brown sugar, cinnamon and cloves in medium bowl.
Cut in butter with a pastry blender or 2 knives until crumbly. Stir
in pumpkin, walnuts and raisins.

ROLL bread dough into 12 x 12-inch square;* spread with
pumpkin mixture, leaving 1-inch border along 2 sides. Roll up
dough, starting from side with 1-inch border; seal edges. Slice into
12 pieces; place cut sides up in greased 9-inch round or square
baking pan. Let rise in warm place until double in size.

BAKE in preheated 375°F. oven for 20 to 25 minutes or until
golden brown. Cool slightly on wire rack. Drizzle with Glaze. Serve
warm. Makes 1 dozen rolls.

For Glaze:
COMBINE 1 cup sifted powdered sugar and 2 to 3 tablespoons
water in small bowl until smooth.

*Note: For extra large rolls, roll dough into 12 x 9-inch rectangle.
Spread with pumpkin mixture, leaving 1-inch border along 9-inch
sides. Roll up dough, starting from 9-inch side; seal edges. Slice
into 6 pieces; place cut sides up in greased 9-inch baking pan. Let
rise and bake as above. Makes 6 rolls.

Also pictured on pages 206 and 207.

golden herb rolls

⅔ cup milk

½ cup (1 stick) butter or margarine

¼ cup water

4 cups all-purpose flour, *divided*

⅓ cup granulated sugar

1 package quick-rising yeast

2 teaspoons dried savory leaves, crushed

1 teaspoon salt

¾ teaspoon dried thyme leaves, crushed

½ teaspoon dried dill weed, crushed

1 cup LIBBY'S® Solid Pack Pumpkin

4 eggs, *divided*

2 tablespoons sesame seeds

COMBINE milk, butter and water in small saucepan; heat until butter is melted. If necessary, cool to 120°F. to 130°F. Combine *3 cups* flour, sugar, yeast, savory, salt, thyme and dill in large mixer bowl. Add milk mixture and pumpkin; beat for 2 minutes. Stir in *3 eggs* and *remaining* flour.

COVER; let rise in warm, draft-free place for 10 minutes or until doubled. Spoon into 20 to 24 well-greased muffin cups, filling ½ to ¾ full. Cover; let rise in warm, draft-free place for 30 to 40 minutes or until doubled. Beat *remaining* egg and brush on top of rolls; sprinkle with sesame seeds.

BAKE in preheated 350°F. oven for 30 to 40 minutes or until golden and rolls sound hollow when tapped. Remove from pans; serve warm, or cool on wire rack. Makes 20 to 24 rolls.

pumpkin marmalade bread

2¼ cups all-purpose flour
¾ cup packed brown sugar
¾ cup granulated sugar
4½ teaspoons pumpkin pie spice
2¼ teaspoons baking powder
¾ teaspoon ground cinnamon
¼ teaspoon salt
1¼ cups LIBBY'S® Solid Pack Pumpkin
4 eggs
½ cup (1 stick) butter or margarine, melted
⅓ cup orange marmalade
3 tablespoons orange liqueur or orange juice
Marmalade Glaze (recipe follows)

COMBINE flour, brown sugar, granulated sugar, pumpkin pie spice, baking powder, cinnamon and salt in medium bowl. Beat pumpkin, eggs, butter, marmalade and liqueur in a large mixer bowl until blended. Gradually beat in flour mixture.

SPREAD batter into greased 9 x 5-inch loaf pan. Bake in preheated 350°F. oven for 65 to 70 minutes or until wooden pick inserted in center comes out clean. Cool in pan on wire rack for 10 minutes; remove to wire rack to cool completely. Spread with Marmalade Glaze. Makes 1 loaf.

For Marmalade Glaze:
MIX 2 tablespoons orange marmalade and 1 tablespoon orange liqueur or orange juice in small bowl.

Pictured on page 217.

old-fashioned nut loaf

2 cups all-purpose flour
2 teaspoons baking powder
2 teaspoons pumpkin pie spice
1 teaspoon salt
½ teaspoon baking soda
1½ cups LIBBY'S® Solid Pack Pumpkin
½ cup granulated sugar
½ cup packed brown sugar
½ cup NESTLÉ® CARNATION® Evaporated Skimmed Milk
1 egg
1 egg white
1 tablespoon vegetable oil
¼ cup chopped nuts

COMBINE flour, baking powder, pumpkin pie spice, salt and baking soda in medium bowl. Combine pumpkin, granulated sugar, brown sugar, evaporated skimmed milk, egg, egg white and vegetable oil in large bowl. Stir in flour mixture until just moistened. Spread batter into greased 9 x 5-inch loaf pan. Sprinkle batter with nuts.

BAKE in preheated 350°F. oven for 60 to 65 minutes or until wooden pick inserted in center comes out clean. Cool in pan on wire rack for 10 minutes. Remove to wire rack to cool completely. Makes 1 loaf (16 slices). Per slice: 2.5 grams fat and 150 calories.

Pictured on page 217.

iced nut and pumpkin loaf

1¾ cups all-purpose flour
½ cup pecans, finely chopped or ground
2¼ teaspoons pumpkin pie spice
1 teaspoon baking soda
½ teaspoon salt
1 cup (2 sticks) butter or margarine, softened
¾ cup granulated sugar
½ cup packed brown sugar
3 eggs
1 cup LIBBY'S® Solid Pack Pumpkin
Icing (recipe follows)

COMBINE flour, pecans, pumpkin pie spice, baking soda and salt in medium bowl. Beat butter, granulated sugar and brown sugar in large mixer bowl until creamy. Beat in eggs until light and fluffy. Gradually beat in pumpkin and flour mixture.

POUR into greased and floured 9 x 5-inch loaf pan. Bake in preheated 325°F. oven for 1 hour and 15 minutes or until wooden pick inserted in center comes out clean. Cool in pan on wire rack for 10 minutes; remove to wire rack to cool completely.

SPREAD Icing over top of loaf, allowing some to drizzle down sides.* Makes 1 loaf.

For Icing:
COMBINE 1¼ cups sifted powdered sugar and 3 to 4 teaspoons water in small bowl.

*Note: To make design, place 2 tablespoons Icing in small heavy-duty plastic bag. Tint with 1 drop maple flavoring or vanilla extract; knead until blended. Cut a small hole in corner of bag; squeeze to drizzle over loaf in crisscross design.

Top to bottom: Old-Fashioned Nut Loaf (see recipe, page 215), Iced Nut and Pumpkin Loaf (see recipe above) and Pumpkin Marmalade Bread (see recipe, page 214)

Quick Bread Savvy

With today's busy schedules, a quick bread is a smart choice whenever you want the fresh-from-the-oven goodness of homemade bread. With these helpful hints, you can enjoy scrumptious loaves and coffeecakes that look and taste as if they were made by an expert.

Start by measuring the ingredients accurately. Successful quick breads depend on the right amounts of ingredients. Too much or too little flour, liquid or leavening may cause trouble.

When you add the liquid ingredients to the dry ones, don't mix the batter too much. Stir only until the dry ingredients are just moistened with some tiny lumps. If you overmix, the bread may be tough and have tunnels.

Once the batter is in the pan, put it in the oven right away. Batters with baking powder and/or baking soda should be baked immediately or the leavening power will be lost.

Check the bread 10 to 15 minutes before the end of the baking. If the bread seems to be browning too quickly, cover it lightly with foil. A crack down the center of a loaf is typical and shows that the batter has risen properly.

To test if a quick bread is done, insert a wooden pick near the center of the bread. If the pick comes out clean, the bread is done. If not, bake it a few minutes more and test again.

Cool a quick bread in the pan on a wire rack about 10 minutes. Then, remove it from the pan and continue cooling it on the rack. The rack allows air to circulate under the bread so it won't become soggy.

While a coffeecake is best served warm, a quick bread loaf improves with standing. If you let it stand overnight, the flavors will have a chance to mellow, and the bread won't crumble when you slice it. After baking, let the loaf cool completely on a wire rack. Wrap it tightly in foil and store it overnight at room temperature. For longer storage, keep it in the refrigerator for up to a week. You can freeze a quick bread for up to 3 months. Place the completely cooled loaf in a freezer container or bag. Before serving, thaw the wrapped loaf overnight in the refrigerator.

sour cream
pumpkin coffeecake

STREUSEL
- ½ cup packed brown sugar
- 1 teaspoon ground cinnamon
- ¼ teaspoon ground allspice
- 2 teaspoons butter or margarine

BATTER
- 3 cups all-purpose flour
- 1 tablespoon ground cinnamon

- 2 teaspoons baking soda
- 1 teaspoon salt
- 1 cup (2 sticks) butter or margarine, softened
- 2 cups granulated sugar
- 4 eggs
- 1 cup LIBBY'S® Solid Pack Pumpkin
- 1 cup sour cream
- 2 teaspoons vanilla extract

For Streusel:
COMBINE brown sugar, cinnamon and allspice in small bowl. Cut in butter with pastry blender or 2 knives until mixture is crumbly.

For Batter:
COMBINE flour, cinnamon, baking soda and salt in medium bowl. Beat butter and granulated sugar in large mixer bowl until light and fluffy. Beat in eggs, one at a time, beating well after each addition.

BEAT in pumpkin, sour cream and vanilla extract. Gradually beat in the flour mixture.

SPOON *half* of the batter into a greased 12-cup fluted tube pan. Sprinkle Streusel over batter, making sure Streusel *does not* touch side of pan. Top with *remaining* batter, making sure batter layer touches side of pan.

BAKE in preheated 350°F. oven for 55 to 60 minutes or until wooden pick comes out clean. Cool in pan on wire rack for 30 minutes. Invert onto rack to cool. Makes 16 servings.

pumpkin streusel coffeecake

STREUSEL TOPPING
- ½ cup all-purpose flour
- ¼ cup packed brown sugar
- 1½ teaspoons ground cinnamon
- 3 tablespoons butter or margarine
- ½ cup coarsely chopped nuts

COFFEECAKE
- 2 cups all-purpose flour
- 2 teaspoons baking powder
- 1½ teaspoons ground cinnamon
- ½ teaspoon baking soda
- ¼ teaspoon salt
- 1 cup (2 sticks) butter or margarine, softened
- 1 cup granulated sugar
- 2 eggs
- 1 cup LIBBY'S® Solid Pack Pumpkin
- 1 teaspoon vanilla extract

For Streusel Topping:
COMBINE flour, brown sugar and cinnamon in medium bowl. Cut in butter with pastry blender or 2 knives until mixture is crumbly; stir in nuts.

For Coffeecake:
COMBINE flour, baking powder, cinnamon, baking soda and salt in small bowl. Beat butter and granulated sugar in large mixer bowl until creamy. Add eggs, one at a time, beating well after each addition. Beat in pumpkin and vanilla extract. Gradually beat in flour mixture.

SPOON *half* of batter into greased and floured 9-inch round cake pan. Sprinkle ¾ *cup* Streusel Topping over batter. Spoon *remaining* batter evenly over Streusel Topping; sprinkle with *remaining* Streusel Topping.

BAKE in preheated 350°F. oven for 45 to 50 minutes or until wooden pick inserted in center comes out clean. Cool in pan on wire rack for 15 minutes; serve warm. Makes 10 servings.

pumpkin oatmeal muffins

1½ cups all-purpose flour
½ cup quick or old-fashioned oats
½ cup chopped walnuts
2 teaspoons baking powder
2 teaspoons pumpkin pie spice
½ teaspoon baking soda
½ teaspoon salt
1 cup LIBBY'S® Solid Pack Pumpkin
2 eggs
½ cup honey
⅓ cup apple juice
¼ cup vegetable oil
2 tablespoons quick or old-fashioned oats

COMBINE flour, ½ cup oats, walnuts, baking powder, pumpkin pie spice, baking soda and salt in large bowl.

COMBINE pumpkin, eggs, honey, apple juice and vegetable oil in medium bowl. Add to flour mixture; stir just until blended. Spoon into 12 greased or paper-lined muffin cups. Sprinkle with 2 tablespoons oats.

BAKE in preheated 375°F. oven for 23 to 27 minutes or until wooden pick inserted in center comes out clean. Remove muffins to wire rack; cool slightly. Serve warm. Makes 1 dozen.

pumpkin corn muffins

1¼ cups all-purpose flour
  1 cup ALBERS® Yellow Corn Meal
⅓ cup granulated sugar
  4 teaspoons baking powder
½ teaspoon salt
1¼ cups LIBBY'S® Solid Pack Pumpkin
  2 eggs
⅓ cup milk
¼ cup vegetable oil

COMBINE flour, cornmeal, sugar, baking powder and salt in large bowl. Beat pumpkin, eggs, milk and vegetable oil in medium bowl. Add to flour mixture; mix well. Spoon into 12 greased or paper-lined muffin cups. Bake in preheated 375°F. oven for 25 to 30 minutes or until wooden pick inserted in center comes out clean. Remove to wire rack; cool slightly. Serve warm. Makes 1 dozen.

Pictured on page 225.

Mighty Good Muffins

Go ahead and splurge! Treat yourself to warm muffins right from the oven. To help you bake the best muffins possible, remember these helpful suggestions:

Use a light hand when you mix the muffin batter. If you overmix, the muffins may have peaked tops, tunnels inside and a tough texture.

Avoid crusty rims around the edges of muffins by greasing the muffin cups on the bottoms and only halfway up the sides.

Muffins are done when they have golden tops and a wooden pick inserted in the center comes out clean. Remove to wire rack; cool slightly.

Store cooled muffins in a plastic bag at room temperature for up to three days. Or, place them in freezer bags and freeze for up to 3 months. To reheat frozen muffins, wrap them in foil and bake in a 300°F. oven for 12 to 15 minutes for 1¾-inch muffins or 15 to 18 minutes for 2½-inch ones.

pumpkin apricot muffins

1⅔ cups all-purpose flour
1 tablespoon baking powder
¾ teaspoon ground cinnamon
¼ teaspoon salt
1 cup LIBBY'S® Solid Pack Pumpkin
¾ cup milk
2 eggs
½ cup packed brown sugar
½ cup dried apricots, chopped
¼ cup (½ stick) butter or margarine, melted
Streusel Topping (recipe follows)

COMBINE flour, baking powder, cinnamon and salt in medium bowl. Mix pumpkin, milk, eggs, brown sugar, apricots and butter in small bowl; add to flour mixture and stir just until moistened. Spoon into 12 greased or paper-lined muffin cups. Sprinkle with Streusel Topping.

BAKE in preheated 375°F. oven for 20 to 25 minutes or until wooden pick inserted in center comes out clean. Remove to wire rack; cool slightly. Serve warm. Makes 1 dozen.

For Streusel Topping:
COMBINE 3 tablespoons finely chopped walnuts, 2 tablespoons granulated sugar and ⅛ teaspoon ground cinnamon in small bowl.

Pumpkin Apricot Muffins (see recipe above) and
Pumpkin Corn Muffins (see recipe, page 223)

pumpkin blueberry streusel muffins

2½ cups all-purpose flour
2 cups granulated sugar
1 tablespoon pumpkin pie spice
1 teaspoon baking soda
½ teaspoon salt
2 eggs
1 cup LIBBY'S® Solid Pack Pumpkin
½ cup vegetable oil
1 cup fresh or frozen blueberries
Streusel Topping (recipe follows)

COMBINE flour, sugar, pumpkin pie spice, baking soda and salt in large bowl. Combine eggs, pumpkin and oil in medium bowl; stir into flour mixture just until moistened. Fold in blueberries. Spoon batter into 18 greased or paper-lined muffin cups, filling ¾ full. Sprinkle with Streusel Topping.

BAKE in preheated 350°F. oven for 30 to 35 minutes or until wooden pick inserted in center comes out clean. Cool in pans on wire racks. Makes 18 muffins.

For Streusel Topping:
COMBINE ⅓ cup granulated sugar, 3 tablespoons all-purpose flour and ½ teaspoon ground cinnamon in medium bowl. Cut in 2 tablespoons butter with pastry blender or 2 knives until mixture is crumbly.

orange brunch muffins

3 cups buttermilk baking mix

¾ cup all-purpose flour

⅔ cup granulated sugar

2 eggs, lightly beaten

½ cup plain yogurt

½ cup orange juice

1 tablespoon grated orange peel

2 cups (12-ounce package) NESTLÉ® TOLL HOUSE® Premier White Morsels, *divided*

½ cup chopped macadamia nuts or walnuts

COMBINE baking mix, flour and sugar in large bowl. Add eggs, yogurt, orange juice and orange peel; stir just until blended. Stir in 1⅓ *cups* morsels. Spoon into 12 to 14 paper-lined muffin cups. Sprinkle with nuts.

BAKE in preheated 375°F. oven for 18 to 22 minutes or until wooden pick inserted in center comes out clean. Cool in pans on wire rack for 10 minutes; remove to wire rack to cool slightly.

PLACE *remaining* morsels in heavy-duty plastic bag. Microwave on MEDIUM-HIGH (70%) power for 1 minute; knead bag to mix. Microwave at additional 10- to 20-second intervals, kneading until smooth. Cut a small hole in corner of bag; squeeze to drizzle chocolate over muffins while still slightly warm. Serve warm. Makes 12 to 14 muffins.

nutty pumpkin waffles

2 cups all-purpose flour
¼ cup granulated sugar
1 tablespoon cornstarch
2 teaspoons baking powder
2 teaspoons ground cinnamon
½ teaspoon salt
¼ teaspoon ground ginger
¼ teaspoon ground nutmeg
1¾ cups milk
½ cup LIBBY'S® Solid Pack Pumpkin
2 eggs, separated
2 tablespoons butter or margarine, melted
¾ cup chopped nuts
Pumpkin Maple Sauce (recipe follows)
Chopped nuts (optional)

COMBINE flour, sugar, cornstarch, baking powder, cinnamon, salt, ginger and nutmeg in large bowl. Combine milk, pumpkin and egg yolks in medium bowl; mix well. Add to flour mixture. Stir in butter. Beat egg whites in small mixer bowl on high speed until soft peaks form. Gently fold into pumpkin mixture.

PREHEAT waffle iron according to manufacturer's directions. Depending on size of waffle iron, pour ½ cup to 1½ cups batter onto hot iron. Generously sprinkle with nuts. Cook for 4 to 5 minutes or until steaming stops. Repeat with remaining batter and nuts. Serve with Pumpkin Maple Sauce. Sprinkle with additional nuts. Makes eight 7-inch waffles.

For Pumpkin Maple Sauce:
HEAT 1 cup maple syrup, ¾ cup LIBBY'S® Solid Pack Pumpkin and ¼ teaspoon ground cinnamon in small saucepan until warm.

pumpkin scones

2½ cups all-purpose flour
¼ cup packed brown sugar
1 tablespoon baking powder
1 teaspoon ground cinnamon
½ teaspoon salt
¼ teaspoon ground cloves
½ cup shortening
¾ cup LIBBY'S® Solid Pack Pumpkin
½ cup milk

COMBINE flour, brown sugar, baking powder, cinnamon, salt and cloves in large bowl. Cut in shortening with pastry blender or 2 knives until mixture resembles coarse crumbs. Combine pumpkin and milk in small bowl. Add to flour mixture; mix just until dough forms.

KNEAD dough gently on floured surface 10 to 12 times. Pat *half* of dough into one 7-inch circle; cut into 6 to 8 wedges. Repeat with *remaining* dough. Place wedges 2 inches apart on ungreased baking sheet.

BAKE in preheated 450°F. oven for 12 to 14 minutes or until light golden color. Remove scones to wire rack; cool slightly. Serve warm. Makes 12 to 16 scones.

pumpkin apple butter

1¾ cups (15-ounce can) LIBBY'S® Solid Pack Pumpkin
  1 cup apple juice
  1 cup peeled and grated apple (about 1 medium)
  ½ cup packed brown sugar
  ¾ teaspoon pumpkin pie spice

COMBINE pumpkin, apple juice, apple, brown sugar and pumpkin pie spice in 2-quart saucepan. Bring to a boil; reduce heat. Simmer, uncovered, for 1½ hours, stirring occasionally. Cool thoroughly; transfer to covered storage container. Store in refrigerator for up to 2 months. Makes 3 cups.

Pumpkin Scones (see recipe opposite) and
Pumpkin Apple Butter (see recipe above)

fiesta corn bread

2¼ cups all-purpose flour
1¾ cups ALBERS® Corn Meal
1½ cups (6 ounces) shredded cheddar cheese
1 cup (7-ounce can) ORTEGA® Diced Green Chiles
½ cup granulated sugar
2 tablespoons baking powder
1½ teaspoons salt
2 cups milk
⅔ cup vegetable oil
2 eggs, lightly beaten

COMBINE flour, cornmeal, cheese, chiles, sugar, baking powder and salt in large bowl. Add milk, oil and eggs; stir just until moistened. Spread into greased 13 x 9-inch baking pan.

BAKE in preheated 375°F. oven for 30 to 35 minutes or until wooden pick inserted in center comes out clean. Cool in pan for 10 minutes; cut into squares. Cut squares diagonally in half. Makes 24 servings.

southwestern biscuits

2¼ cups all-purpose flour
2 tablespoons granulated sugar
1 tablespoon baking powder
3 tablespoons butter or margarine, softened
1 egg
1 cup (8-ounce can) cream-style corn
½ cup (4-ounce can) ORTEGA® Diced Green Chiles
1 tablespoon chopped fresh cilantro (optional)

COMBINE flour, sugar and baking powder in large bowl. Add butter; cut in with pastry blender or 2 knives until mixture resembles coarse crumbs.

STIR IN egg, corn, chiles and cilantro; combine just until mixture holds together. Knead dough 10 times on well-floured surface. Pat dough to ¾-inch thickness. Cut into 3-inch biscuits. Place on greased baking sheets.

BAKE in preheated 400°F. oven for 20 to 25 minutes or until wooden pick inserted in center comes out clean. Cool on baking sheets for 5 minutes; remove to wire racks to cool completely. Makes about 8 biscuits.

Bake a Better Biscuit

Making light, tender and flaky biscuits is easy if you remember these basics:

Cut in the butter or margarine just until the flour mixture resembles coarse crumbs. Then, stir in the liquid only until the ingredients are just moistened.

Knead the dough lightly by folding and pressing only enough to distribute the liquid; 10 strokes is plenty.

Cut out as many biscuits as possible from the first rolling of dough. Additional rolling and extra flour will make the biscuits tough and dry.

Place biscuits close together on the baking sheet for a soft crust; for a firmer crust, place them about 1 inch apart.

baking basics

If you know the basics, you can master the skill of baking. Here are some baking tips, plus step-by-step instructions for melting chocolate, that will help you bake and decorate everything from the simplest cookies to the most elaborate desserts.

butter & margarine

For baking, the Nestlé Culinary Center suggests using butter or regular stick margarine for the best results. However, if you prefer using a lower-fat margarine, choose one with no less than 60% vegetable oil. Products labeled as "spread" and "diet" contain less fat and more water. They tend to produce a cookie that is more cakelike and less crisp around the edges.

masterful melting

The key to melting chocolate successfully is to use slow and gentle heat.

Melting Larger Amounts

To melt NESTLÉ® TOLL HOUSE® Semi-Sweet Chocolate Morsels or broken-up Semi-Sweet or Unsweetened Chocolate Baking Bars, microwave 1 cup (6 ounces) in an uncovered microwave-safe bowl on HIGH (100%) power for 1 minute; stir. Microwave at additional 10- to 20-second intervals, stirring until smooth.

For the more delicate products—Milk Chocolate Morsels, Butterscotch Morsels, Premier White Morsels or Premier White Baking Bars—melt as above, except use MEDIUM-HIGH (70%) power.

Or, melt morsels or baking bars in a *heavy-duty* saucepan on *lowest possible* heat. When chocolate begins to melt and become shiny, remove from heat; stir. Return to heat for a few seconds at a time, stirring until smooth. (This method is not recommended for more delicate morsels and baking bars.)

Dazzle with a Drizzle

A drizzle of white "chocolate" adds a pastry-shop touch to cookies, brownies, cakes, fudge and truffles. Place ½ cup NESTLÉ® TOLL HOUSE® Premier White Morsels or 2 bars (2 ounces *each*) NESTLÉ® TOLL HOUSE® Premier White Baking Bar in a heavy-duty plastic bag. Microwave on MEDIUM-HIGH (70%) power for 45 seconds; knead bag to mix. Microwave at additional 10- to 20-second intervals, kneading until smooth. (Semi-sweet chocolate morsels and baking bars may be melted in the same way, using HIGH (100%) power.)

Cut a small hole in the corner of the bag; squeeze to drizzle. For a thicker or thinner drizzle, adjust the size of the hole you cut in the bag.

equipment

Use these tips when considering mixing equipment and bakeware:

Consider a portable electric mixer (hand-held mixer) for light jobs and short mixing periods. For heavy-duty jobs and long mixing periods, use a freestanding electric mixer.

The material bakeware is made from—aluminum, tin, stainless steel, black steel or pottery—and the finish it has influence the quality of baked products. Shiny bakeware reflects heat, making the browning process slower, while dark bakeware and bakeware with a dull finish absorb more heat, increasing browning of baked goods.

measuring

Not all ingredients are measured the same way, so keep this measuring guide handy when baking:

Measuring spoons are different from the ones you use for eating. Generally, these spoons come in a set that includes 1-tablespoon, 1-teaspoon, ½-teaspoon and ¼-teaspoon sizes. Use measuring spoons to measure small amounts of both liquid and dry ingredients.

When measuring liquids of ¼ cup or larger, use a standard glass or clear plastic liquid measuring cup. Place the cup on a level surface; bend down so your eye is level with the marking you wish to read. Fill the cup up to the marking. Do not lift the cup off the counter to your eye while measuring; your hand is not as steady as the countertop.

When measuring dry ingredients, use a dry measuring cup that is the exact capacity you wish to measure. These individual cups usually come in sets, including 1-cup, ½-cup, ⅓-cup and ¼-cup sizes. Using a spoon, lightly pile the ingredient into the cup. Then, using a metal spatula, level off the measure. Never pack dry ingredients except brown sugar. Pack brown sugar into the cup so it holds the shape of the measuring cup.

Is sifting necessary? All-purpose flour is no longer lumpy and compact like the flour of yesteryear. That's why stirring it before measuring is sufficient. Stirring works well for most other flours also, except cake flour, which has a very soft texture and tends to pack down. We recommend that you sift cake flour to remove any lumps and to lighten it before measuring.

A dash is a measure of less than ⅛ teaspoon. To get a dash, just add a quick shake or a sprinkle of the ingredient. When a dash is used, it's usually for flavor; the actual amount is up to you.

oven tips

When monitoring oven temperature, use an oven thermometer. Since temperature variances of up to 25°F. are quite common, it's a good idea to check the internal temperature of your oven before baking. If the temperature is too high or low, adjust the settings accordingly.

Preheating the oven will give you the best results when making baked goods. All recipe timings in this cookbook are based on a preheated oven.

If the appearance or texture of a baked product does not seem correct, review the oven manufacturer's instructions for the proper procedure in preheating your oven. Also, after preheating your oven, double-check the oven's internal temperature with an oven thermometer.

index

index

metric cooking hints

Metric Cooking Hints

By making a few conversions, cooks in Australia, Canada, and the United Kingdom can use the recipes in *Nestlé® Best-Ever Cookies* with confidence. The charts on this page provide a guide for converting measurements from the U.S. customary system, which is used throughout this book, to the imperial and metric systems. There also is a conversion table for oven temperatures to accommodate the differences in oven calibrations.

Product Differences: Most of the ingredients called for in the recipes in this book are available in English-speaking countries. However, some are known by different names. Here are some common American ingredients and their possible counterparts:
■ Sugar is granulated or castor sugar.
■ Powdered sugar is icing sugar.
■ All-purpose flour is plain household flour or white flour. When self-rising flour is used in place of all-purpose flour in a recipe that calls for leavening, omit the leavening agent (baking soda or baking powder) and salt.
■ Light corn syrup is golden syrup.
■ Cornstarch is cornflour.
■ Baking soda is bicarbonate of soda.
■ Vanilla is vanilla essence.
■ Green, red, or yellow sweet peppers are capsicums.
■ Golden raisins are sultanas.

Volume and Weight: Americans traditionally use cup measures for liquid and solid ingredients. The chart, below, shows the approximate imperial and metric equivalents. If you are accustomed to weighing solid ingredients, the following approximate equivalents will be helpful.
■ 1 cup butter, castor sugar, or rice = 8 ounces = about 250 grams
■ 1 cup flour = 4 ounces = about 125 grams
■ 1 cup icing sugar = 5 ounces = about 150 grams
   Spoon measures are used for smaller amounts of ingredients. Although the size of the tablespoon varies slightly in different countries, for practical purposes and for recipes in this book, a straight substitution is all that's necessary.
   Measurements made using cups or spoons always should be level unless stated otherwise.

Equivalents: U.S. = Australia/U.K.

⅛ teaspoon = 0.5 ml
¼ teaspoon = 1 ml
½ teaspoon = 2 ml
1 teaspoon = 5 ml
1 tablespoon = 1 tablespoon
¼ cup = 2 tablespoons = 2 fluid ounces = 60 ml
⅓ cup = ¼ cup = 3 fluid ounces = 90 ml
½ cup = ⅓ cup = 4 fluid ounces = 120 ml
⅔ cup = ½ cup = 5 fluid ounces = 150 ml
¾ cup = ⅔ cup = 6 fluid ounces = 180 ml
1 cup = ¾ cup = 8 fluid ounces = 240 ml
1¼ cups = 1 cup
2 cups = 1 pint
1 quart = 1 liter
½ inch =1.27 cm
1 inch = 2.54 cm

Baking Pan Sizes

American	Metric
8 x 1½-inch round baking pan	20 x 4-cm cake tin
9 x 1½-inch round baking pan	23 x 3.5-cm cake tin
11 x 7 x 1½-inch baking pan	28 x 18 x 4-cm baking tin
13 x 9 x 2-inch baking pan	30 x 20 x 3-cm baking tin
2-quart rectangular baking dish	30 x 20 x 3-cm baking tin
15 x 10 x 1-inch baking pan	30 x 25 x 2-cm baking tin (Swiss roll tin)
9-inch pie plate	22 x 4- or 23 x 4-cm pie plate
7- or 8-inch springform pan	18- or 20-cm springform or loose-bottom cake tin
9 x 5 x 3-inch loaf pan	23 x 13 x 7-cm or 2-pound narrow loaf tin or pâté tin
1½-quart casserole	1.5-liter casserole
2-quart casserole	2-liter casserole

Oven Temperature Equivalents

Fahrenheit Setting	Celsius Setting*	Gas Setting
300°F	150°C	Gas Mark 2 (slow)
325°F	160°C	Gas Mark 3 (moderately slow)
350°F	180°C	Gas Mark 4 (moderate)
375°F	190°C	Gas Mark 5 (moderately hot)
400°F	200°C	Gas Mark 6 (hot)
425°F	220°C	Gas Mark 7
450°F	230°C	Gas Mark 8 (very hot)
Broil		Grill

*Electric and gas ovens may be calibrated using Celsius. However, for an electric oven, increase the Celsius setting 10 to 20 degrees when cooking above 160°C. For convection or forced-air ovens (gas or electric), lower the temperature setting 10°C when cooking at all heat levels.